RENAISSANCE FLORENCE
The Age of Lorenzo de' Medici
1449-1492

RENAISSANCE FLORENCE

The Age of Lorenzo de' Medici
1449–1492

edited by
Cristina Acidini Luchinat

CHARTA

Catalogue

Design
Gabriele Nason

Editorial coordination
Emanuela Belloni

Layout and editing
Ready-made, Milano

Press office
Silvia Palombi

Typesetting
Type srl, Sesto San Giovanni, Milan

Technical realization / Production
Amilcare Pizzi Arti grafiche,
Cinisello Balsamo, Milan

Printed in Italy by Amilcare Pizzi
ISBN 88-86158-45-9

Under the Gracious Patronage of
His Excellency Oscar Luigi Scalfaro
President of the Italian Republic

Renaissance Florence
The Age of Lorenzo de' Medici
(1449-1492)

London, Accademia Italiana
delle Arti e delle Arti Applicate

14th October 1993 - 23rd January 1994

in co-operation with

the Italian Ministry of Foreign
Affairs

The Exhibition is Sponsored by

American Express Foundation

The catalogue has been published
thanks to the generous support of

Honorary Committee

Beniamino Andreatta
Italian Minister of Foreign Affairs
Alberto Ronchey
Italian Minister of Cultural Heritage

Valdo Spini, *Chairman Honorary*
Committee
Italian Minister of the Environment
Chairman of the Executive Committee
for the Celebrations in Honour of the
Fifth Centenary of the Death of
Lorenzo the Magnificent

Laura Fincato
Under Secretary
Italian Ministry of Cultural Heritage
Bruno Bottai
Secretary General
Italian Ministry of Foreign Affairs
Giacomo Attolico
Italian Ambassador, London
Giorgio Morales
Mayor of Florence
Alessandro Vattani
Director General of Cultural
Relations
Italian Ministry of Foreign Affairs
Francesco Sisinni
Director General, Central Department
B.A.A.A.A.S.
Italian Ministry of Cultural Heritage
Antonio Paolucci
Superintendent for Artistic and
Historic Heritage of Florence
Rosalia Mannu Tolu
Superintendent for Archives of
Florence
Francesco Nicosia
Superintendent for Archaeology of
Florence
Susan S. Bloom
Vice President Cultural Affairs,
American Express Company
Lapo Mazzei
Chairman, Cassa di Risparmio di
Firenze

Steering Committee

Cristina Acidini
Vice Superintendent of the
Superintendency for Artistic and
Historic Heritage of Florence
Antonio Armellini
Minister-Counsellor, Italian Embassy,
London
Maria Grazia Benini
Head of Department VII, Central
Office B.A.A.A.S.
Italian Ministry Cultural Heritage
Roberta Cremoncini
Accademia Italiana, London
Luciana Di Leo
Accademia Italiana, London
Maurizio di Puolo
"Studio Metaimago", Rome
Jane Drew
Manager Public Affairs, American
Express, Europe Ltd.
Elisabetta Kelescian
Italian Consul General, Barcelona
Rosa Maria Letts
Chairman, Accademia Italiana,
London
Ombretta Pacilio
Head of Department III,
General Department of Cultural
Relations
Italian Ministry of Foreign Affairs
Michelangelo Pipan
Counsellor for Cultural Affairs,
Italian Embassy, London
Ennio Troili
General Department of Cultural
Relations
Italian Ministry of Foreign Affairs

Curated by
Cristina Acidini
Vice Superintendent of the
Superintendency for Artistic and
Historic Heritage of Florence in
conjunction with the Committee for
the Celebrations in Honour of the
Fifth Centenary of the Death of
Lorenzo the Magnificent

Exhibition designer
Maurizio di Puolo/"Studio
Metaimago" - Rome

Installation
Bourlet-Martin

Insurance
H M Government Indemnity
Crowley Colosso

Transport
Universal Express srl

List of Lenders

Accademia delle Arti e del Disegno, Firenze
Accademia Etrusca di Cortona (Ar)
Archivio di Stato di Firenze
Basilica di San Lorenzo, Firenze
Biblioteca Estense, Modena
Biblioteca Medicea Laurenziana, Firenze
Biblioteca Nazionale Centrale, Firenze
Biblioteca Riccardiana, Firenze
Alberto Bruschi di Grassina (Fi)
Cassa di Risparmio di Firenze
Cattedrale di Santa Maria del Fiore, Firenze
Chiesa dei Sant'Ambrogio, Firenze
Chiesa della Ss. Annunziata, Firenze
Chiesa di San Donato a Certaldo, Firenze
Chiesa di San Michele a San Salvi, Firenze
Chiesa di San Romolo a Tignano, Barberino Val d'Elsa (Fi)
Chiesa di Santa Lucia dei Magnoli, Firenze
Chiesa di Santa Maria nella Badia Fiorentina, Firenze
Chiesa di Santa Trinita, Firenze
Chiesa di Santo Spirito, Firenze
Almastella Fioretto, Firenze
Galleria degli Uffizi, Firenze
Galleria dell'Accademia, Firenze
Galleria dell'Istituto degli Innocenti, Firenze
Galleria Palatina, Firenze
Museo Archeologico di Firenze
Museo Bandini di Fiesole (Fi)
Museo Bardini, Firenze
Museo Civico di Montalcino (Si)
Museo degli Argenti, Firenze
Museo del Tesoro della Basilica di Santa Maria, Impruneta (Fi)
Museo dell'Ateneo Pesarese, Pesaro
Museo dell'Opera del Duomo, Firenze
Museo della Collegiata di Empoli (Fi)
Museo Diocesano, Pistoia
Museo di Casa Buonarroti, Firenze
Museo di Mineralogia e Litologia dell'Università, Firenze
Museo di Palazzo Davanzati, Firenze
Museo di Palazzo Venezia, Roma

Museo di San Domenico, Bologna
Museo di San Marco, Firenze
Museo Internazionale delle Ceramiche, Faenza
Museo Nazionale del Bargello, Firenze
Museo Stibbert, Firenze
Mario Scalini, Firenze
Victoria and Albert Museum, London

The two plastercasts of the *Battle of Lapyths and Centaurs* and of the *Madonna of the Stairs* by Michelangelo have been moulded by the Istituto d'Arte di Porta Romana, Florence.

Acknowledgment
The exhibition has been made possible thanks to the generosity and cooperation of the Comune, Province and Diocese of Florence and all the lenders who include Museums, Churches and Public and Private Intitutions.

The restoration of the Renaissance frame from the Palazzo Davanzati has been made possible through the generous support of FederLegno-Arredo, SpeciaLegno Milan.

Lorenzo il Magnifico (1449-1492)

The celebrations of the fifth centenary of the death of Lorenzo il Magnifico (1449-1492) have exceeded their strictly logical time limit and inspired other international initiatives designed to commemorate Renaissance Florence's *Signore* and his city. *Renaissance Florence: The Age of Lorenzo de' Medici* is a prestigious and important exhibition, bringing to life one of the great periods of the history of art and culture, when Florence could truly be said to be one of the great European capitals of the world as it was then known.

The year 1492 is really quite symbolic. This was the year in which America was discovered, the date conventionally chosen as designating the point at which the Middle Ages gave way to the modern age.

Between 8th April 1992 and 8th April 1993, at least fifty cultural events were organized in Florence by the National Committee for the Celebrations in Honour of the Fifth Centenary of the Death of Lorenzo il Magnifico. These included exhibitions, conferences, tours both of Florentine museums and of the area, and performances – not to mention the restoration works and publications that resulted from all these events (more than thirty of the latter at the last count).

Several works of art were restored for the Laurentian celebrations – these were the famous murals of the *Procession of the Three Magi* painted by candlelight by Benozzo Gozzoli in the chapel of the Medici palace built by the family architect, Michelozzo Michelozzi; Botticelli's *St Ambrose Altarpiece*, the famous statue of the Red Marsyas from the classical Greek period of which Lorenzo was so fond, and Verrocchio's bronze of *The Incredulity of St Thomas*, all of which are in the Uffizi.

Nicolai Rubinstein said in the Palazzo Vecchio on 8th April 1993: "It would clearly be impossible to do justice in just a few words to the enormous success of the exhibitions held during this Laurentian Year...". There have been so many new developments and so many new discoveries, both as regards the objects themselves and as regards their place in the exhibitions, that have excited new ideas and new interpretations.

Unfortunately exhibitions are by their very nature ephemeral, but those who have been lucky enough to visit them will always have the catalogues as reminders, each of which has an important part to play in future Laurentian research by virtue of the enormous amount of material, reproductions and scholarship they contain. This is also true of the conferences – the papers are soon to be published, and these will undoubtedly be seen as milestones in their subject.

Apart from the international conference on *Lorenzo il Magnifico e il Suo Mondo* organized at the Villa I Tatti by the Harvard Center for Italian Renaissance and the Istituto Nazionale di Studi sul Rinascimento, and the seminar on *Il Disegno Fiorentino al Tempo di Lorenzo il Magnifico* at the Villa Spelman, which is part of the John Hopkins University, The Warburg Institute of the University of London and the University of Warwick organized the hugely important *Lorenzo il Magnifico, Cultura e Politica della Firenze Medicea*.

In America as well, the City University of New York's Brooklyn College held a long and erudite conference entitled *Lorenzo de' Medici, Nuove Prospettive*.

Guicciardini described Lorenzo il Magnifico as "the needle on the Italian political scales" because by trying to defend the autonomy of the Florentine *Signoria* within the context of a shattered and divided Italy, he managed to bring equilibrium and stability to the whole of Italy, a period of relative peace and, above all, safety from foreign interferences.

Just a few years after his death, in 1494, it was the internal Italian conflicts that brought about the downfall of his political *chef-d'oeuvre*. That was the year in which Ludovico il Moro, Duke of Milan, called King Charles VIII to Italy, for the advancement of his own expansionist plans. Charles VIII's intervention was not successful, but his incursion into Italy was only the first in a long series of invasions. The story of Lorenzo is thus rechoed in the relatively recent Unification of Italy.

One of the results of Charles VIII's invasion was the fall of the Medici power in Florence (then in the hands of Lorenzo's son Piero) and the creation of the Republic, which finally appeased the followers of the Dominican monk Girolamo Savonarola and their hitherto unsatisfied lust for freedom. Savonarola was one of the great militants of the period who eventually ended his days burnt at the stake in the Piazza della Signoria, in front of the Palazzo Vecchio.

It was Thomas Mann, the great German writer, who wrote the great idealized deathbed scene between Lorenzo and the Dominican friar in his play *Fiorenza*.

Lorenzo, the great prince, the great scholar, and the great promoter of arts and culture was an autocrat, a man with an immensely complex personality.

Machiavelli said of Lorenzo: "There were two separate people in him, almost like an impossible conjunction conjoined", thus synthesizing the contrast between his intellectual self and his role as leader of the Florentine *Signoria*. There can be no better way, however, of describing Lorenzo than in his own words – first the famous joyful ones:

Quant'è bella giovinezza,
Che si fugge tuttavia!
Chi vuol essere lieto, sia:
Di doman non c'è certezza.

Then the words intended to define the tasks that fall to the *Signore*, harsher and more thoughtful:

... Distributore è il Signor vero:
L'Onor ha solo di tal fatica frutto:
L'Onor che ha ogni altra cosa vile,
Ch'e ben gran premio al core alto e gentile
(*Sacra Rappresentazione di San Giovanni e Paolo*, XXXV, 4-8)

These two sets of verses summarize the two sides of Lorenzo's character: on one side the young follower of the Neoplatonist theories, where good finds its way through beauty, and on the other the *Signore*, the Prince who tries to live out a set of values. This very tension between the two sides of Lorenzo will continue to excite fierce debate amongst the intelligentsia and the profane. He was an exemplary figure of the Italian Renaissance who will continue both to pose questions and to incite them.

Valdo Spini
Chairman of the Committee for the Celebrations in Honour of the Fifth Centenary of the Death of Lorenzo il Magnifico

In 1980, under the aegis of the Council of Europe, the exhibition *Firenze e la Toscana dei Medici nell'Europa del '500* was held in Florence.

This was an exhibition which approached the subject from a different, historical point of view, for the series of exhibitions previously mounted had concentrated on stylistic and artistic matters. All aspects of civil life in those times were covered: culture and historical documents, the figurative and decorative arts and the architecture of the city and area. There was also a series of small sister exhibitions in each of the centres of what had once been the Medici state, in addition to the nine held in Florence.

There was a period when a vast number of conferences were held, researches undertaken and books published on the Renaissance and Mannerism, all of which, in fact, took rather a diminished view of the Florentine and Italian tradition.

The problem remained, however, of carrying out as much research on the early Medici as had been done on the later ones. The year 1992, the five hundredth anniversary of Lorenzo's death, seemed to suggest itself as propitious for a complementary in-depth and analytical investigation of the 15th century concentrating on Lorenzo il Magnifico's life and pursuing the theme of crisis and uncertainty that extended into Savonarola's brief period of influence, through Leo X's papacy and well into the Roman 16th century. As it is well known, there are essentially two different schools of thought about Lorenzo's character, based on the ambiguity of his nature as described by Machiavelli. On one hand Lorenzo is seen as the 'monumental' symbol of the culmination of the Renaissance, its culture, its poetry, its music and its art, and on the other he is seen as having secretly abused his influential position in the State by having supposedly appropriated public funds for private use in the midst of a growing economic crisis that culminated in the bankruptcy of the Medici Bank shortly after his death. A series of question marks now hangs over the question of his role as patron of the artistic life of the city. Which is to be believed? The myth of Lorenzo that was built up by his biographers or the rather tarnished image thrown up by relatively recent research?

It was now a matter of evaluating Lorenzo's character within its established historical context through a total revision of the available sources.

The exhibition that opens today in London is a representative sample of works, necessarily abridged for reasons of conservation and transportation. It has come together against a great background of study, research, documentation, newspaper articles and meetings, not to mention all the exhibitions held in Florence in 1992.

The exhibition explored the theme of civil and cultural history: the great Florentine libraries, *in primis* the Biblioteca Laurenziana exhibited their treasures, and the Archivio di Stato investigated the content and meaning of the documents. The Diocese of Florence provided an exhibition devoted to the role of the Church and religious piety, and there was also an exhibition on entertainments of the time and the chivalric revival typical of that age. With regard to the figurative arts, the architectural exhibition revealed the magnitude of a cultural project that, in spite of the fact that few buildings were actually erected and none were completed, encompassed both the craftsmanship of Brunelleschi and the lofty Albertian theme of Renaissance classicism, bringing about a new concept of urban design and planning that was no longer restricted to single buildings. The architectural exhibition was intended to make an effective contribution to Laurentian architecture and its recognition throughout the territory, concentrating on less well-known buildings such as the Villa di Ospedaletto outside Pisa. There was also an opportunity to examine the problems presented by the proposed restoration of the Villa di Careggi which, although it was neither built by nor for Lorenzo, was one of the most important buildings of his time by virtue of the fact that he lived and died in it. The figurative arts were represented by a recognition of the magnificent blossoming of Florentine art and design which established it as one of the supreme paradigms of the 15th century through the 'botteghe', which were regarded as training schools, workshops and centres of exchange of style and the expression of the formal language of the great personalities.

There was an exhibition devoted to the laying out of the gardens at San Marco, with precious original notes, showing just how seminal an experience this was for the young Michelangelo. It also attempted to uncover the truth that lies somewhere between the myth and the elusive historical accounts of this hot-house of young artists chosen by Lorenzo. The restoration of Verrocchio's *Incredulity of St Thomas* was the subject of an extensive exhibition, which has also been to the Metropolitan Museum in New York, and which provided an opportunity to research a work of art by Lorenzo's favourite sculptor. Alongside these initiatives were the 'guides' from the Florentine museums intended to interpret those works of art that could not be moved for conservation reasons and others for the surrounding area, which help to give a clearer picture of the Laurentian age, the poetry of nature and landscape that were also reflected in the literature of that time. Thanks to all the foreign cultural institutes in Florence, and prestigious institutions from New York to Berlin, and all the Tuscan universities, there has been a huge leap forward in our understanding of Lorenzo since the fifth centenary of his birth just after the Second World War, when our knowledge of him was rather limited. A huge amount of editorial effort has gone into putting the catalogues together, covering all the different aspects of Laurentian culture from literature to poetry, from civil history to the history of costume and the many faces of its artistic history.

The London exhibition then brings together an unprecedented synthesis of what in Florence had, through necessity to be a series of exhibitions, due to the lack of a sufficiently large and secure exhibition space in Florence – which is a tremendous shortcoming in so prestigious a capital of art – but also by the fact that all the work was delegated, so to speak, to the city's cultural institutions and museums. This is a synthesis that feeds off what Gide would call a '*nourriture terrestre*', imbued with the freshness of newly reviewed and revisited sources, points of view and cultural theses on every subject. The end result is a distillation of a world that never ceases to amaze through its great refinement, complexity and contradictory nature, and the richness of the contributions made by a society that in its entirety, together with the 'chameleon-like' Lorenzo, bears witness to the universality and topicality of the message of the Italian Renaissance.

Franco Borsi
Secretary of the Committee for the Celebrations in Honour of the Fifth Centenary of the Death of Lorenzo il Magnifico

Renaissance Florence: the Age of Lorenzo de' Medici (1449-1492)

Part of the impetus behind our decision to bring at least one exhibition to London in celebration of the five hundredth anniversary of the death of Lorenzo de' Medici was a desire to share this great historical Italian event with the British public.

It was only fitting that the Soprintendenza di Firenze should choose to share this moment of reflection and revaluation of the great Laurentian era with such great lovers of Florence. British, above all nations, have researched, studied and collected the arts and literature of the Florentine Renaissance, and had it not been for our request, the Laurentian commemorative exhibitions would have remained confined to Florence. These exhibitions took up the greater part of 1992 in the Tuscan capital and are beautifully recalled in the preface to the catalogue by Minister Valdo Spini, Chairman of the Honorary Committee.

Our request was born of a conviction that Lorenzo de' Medici was one of the most fascinating characters in Italian history and just as important for the foreign public. With his mixture of ostentation and nonchalance, his religiousness and his lack of scruples, his academic and popular interests, a composer of philosophical and Humanist works, literary poems and carnival songs, Lorenzo gives the impression of being the cultured Italian *par excellence*, as far as foreigners are concerned. His name is linked with those of Pico della Mirandola, Marsilio Ficino and Poliziano. He was also a statesman, however, and, in this context, his name is linked with that of Machiavelli; he was prudent and wise, a peace-maker and a creator of political stability, not a battle hero, while Italy was experiencing her finest hour.

The second half of the Quattrocento was really Italy's sublime moment, when literary, philosophical and political aspirations were allowed to flourish, and the poets and artists of the time could create myths and images that then served to motivate the very patrons who might have inspired them in the first place.

Religious entertainments, as well as comedies and dramas, took place in public, in the churches, in the piazze and in the streets of the city. There has never been another city like Florence: it is intimate, dialectic and earthy, yet refined. Here for the first time in the middle of the 15th century, the seigneurial palaces were completely surrounded by stone seats from which the elderly or the passers-by could stop and observe the daily comings and goings, the processions and the district's festivities. The Signore, Lorenzo himself, often took part in the processions, sometimes up in front on horseback, sometimes among the members of the confraternity responsible for the entertainment, sometimes singing or reciting verses to the accompaniment of a lute at carnival time.

"*And there was a time*" of peace, peace that came about through Lorenzo's act of courage and subjugation, when he presented himself unarmed at the court of the King of Naples. The King was an ally of the Pope, and they both intended to fight Lorenzo. Lorenzo managed to change the King's mind after four months of diplomatic endeavour, and twenty years' peace was guaranteed to the "Bel paese là dove il sì suona".

"*And there was the time*". 'Le temps revient' was Lorenzo's motto, written on a branch of laurel springing to life once more from an old tree trunk. This also applies to Italy and to Florence, to the arts and to the love of study and literature which left such a magnificent bequest to the whole world. Lorenzo's was an era without precedent in terms of sculpture, painting and architecture, not only never bettered, but never forgotten, which is even more important. These achievements have been a constant source of inspiration the worldover. And all this came from one small city, intimate and homely, almost cosy one might say, and family-based. As Lorenzo said: "a city is a collection of families". Against this background of fiery relationships and deeply-rooted loves and hates, the citizens of Florence launched themselves towards the highest levels of human creativity.

It is to this Florence, to the city as a whole, that we owe this poetic exhibition that reveals so much of the life of the city during that period.

In thanking all those who have had a hand in bringing this exhibition together, I would especially like to thank the lenders and the curators who have helped with the choice of the exhibits and who have contributed to the catalogue.

Maurizio di Puolo, the designer, well-known for the installation of countless exhibitions, was responsible for this magnificent *mise-en-scène*. He has been a key figure in the organization of the exhibition, and his contribution has far exceeded that of the installation alone.

It has to be said that the real architect of this "invention" is Cristina Acidini, Deputy Superintendent of the city of Florence. It was she who put together the story and wrote the script, and it is thanks to her expertise that we have been able to zoom in on this highly original slice of life, the times and the court during the age of Lorenzo. Cristina Acidini was one of the curators of the exhibition on the *Maestri e botteghe, Pittura a Firenze alla fine del Quattrocento* and in charge of the restoration of the Medici Chapel. *Renaissance Florence: The Age of Lorenzo de' Medici (1449-1492)* is her story, the story of her people. Her clarity of presentation and mastery of the subject is ample demonstration of this.

Minister Spini, who was the Chairman of the Committee for the Laurentian celebrations and Chairman of our Honorary Committee, was responsible for calling us all to Florence last year right in the middle of a scorching August to discuss and examine the feasibility of this exhibition.

As if conspirators, we then threw ourselves into action. This exhibition is the result.

Rosa Maria Letts
Chairman, Accademia Italiana

Introduction to the Exhibition

The idea of organizing an exhibition outside Italy on the subject of Florentine civilization during the age of Lorenzo il Magnifico had all the makings of a challenge. The Soprintendenza di Firenze was asked by the Accademia Italiana delle Arti e delle Arti Applicate in London, who were mounting the exhibition, to deal with the scientific side of things and to choose the exhibits – and juggling requirements and problems proved to be no easy matter. Soon after our first requests for information and loans from various organisations – museums and churches in particular – were made, it became quite clear that the exhibition would have to be rethought. The idea was to capitalize on the tremendous result of all the exhibitions and conferences held in 1992, in terms of the wealth of information and scholarship, and to present an abridged overview, yet not a narrower one. It was a question of concentrating on some of the most important questions, not all, unfortunately, that could be illustrated and backed up by a well-chosen selection of documents and manuscripts, *objets d'art*, furnishings and collector's pieces. As far as the selection of material went, not all the pieces included in the nine Florentine exhibitions in 1992 were available: some would have been too fragile to be moved or to have undergone the long journey, others were being restored or had been lent to other exhibitions, and there were some that were just too big. The greatest problem was posed by the painted panels (more popular than canvas in 15th century art), which are enormously problematic to move, as conservators in museums the world over are well aware.

The bones of a new exhibition gradually took shape and the question of coherence and availability of the exhibits was evaluated in terms of the equally important question of conservation of the works. It would be an exhibition of predominantly small works, apart from a few large paintings and the sumptuous church hangings, all chosen in view of their historical relevance or their artistic merit. All the exhibits are strictly authentic, dating from the second half of the 15th century or the very beginning of the 16th century: all are original, apart from three copies of works that could absolutely not be moved (not only from Italy but from their usual habitat) but which are enormously relevant to some of the key points, albeit as reproductions. These are the marble reliefs of Michelangelo's *Battle of the Centaurs and his Madonna of the Stairs*, which could not be removed from the Casa Buonarroti but which were vital to the appreciation of the young Michangelo's work in Lorenzo de' Medici's 'Sculpture Garden' at San Marco. Plaster casts of each of these were made especially for this exhibition. Also there is a photograph (as there was in the Florentine architectural exhibition) of the glazed terracotta frieze from the Medici villa at Poggio a Caiano, symbolic of Lorenzo's last years, which is too fragile and unstable to be moved.

The thread of the exhibition, which is followed by the arrangement and dispersal of the exhibits, weaves a historical picture of Florentine society from 1470-1500 in its various forms – political, administrative and religious – culminating in the role of the Medici family in civil life and the power they wielded through the buildings they erected and the territory they oversaw. In the section devoted to art, we have reconstructed *per exempla* the lively world of the Florentine workshops or *botteghe* specialising in painting and the applied arts, against whose varied background the great masters take their place, not as isolated genii but as guides and points of reference for a myriad of minor artists. The few statues and reliefs belong to the syntonic theme of the Gardens of San Marco, which was a hot-house for young artists chosen by Lorenzo il Magnifico to serve their sculpture and design apprenticeships there; and finally there is a glimpse into Lorenzo's private antiques and library collections: rare and exquisite archaeological pieces and a well-chosen selection of manuscripts.

We were well aware of the limitations and lacunae inherent in any attempt, at a distance of five centuries, to recapture the public and private life of mythical Renaissance Florence, giving particular emphasis to the elusive and contradictory personality of Lorenzo de' Medici, by means of documents and objects. The humanities and the arts, philosophy and music are represented by a few, indirectly related exhibits. The technique for fortifications, which was so greatly developed during the age of Lorenzo, has had to remain in the shadows simply because of the space the models and reconstructions would have required. Missing too, and unfortunately so, are the many very skilled drawings from the highly scientific exhibition organised in Florence by the Gabinetto Disegni e Stampe at the Uffizi; but in the wake of the bombing on 27th May it is quite understandable that the amount of restoration and reconstruction being undertaken by the Galleries prevented their being loaned. (An extraordinary exception is thus represented by the loan of Fra Bartolomeo's two small side panels which are used in a reconstruction of Del Pugliese's tabernacle, alongside the Dudley *Madonna* from the Victoria & Albert Museum.) Draughtsmanship played such a vital part in the apprenticeship and working life of the Renaissance artists and the quality of work produced by masters such as Lippi, Verrocchio, Botticelli and Leonardo da Vinci was so high that this might well be the subject of a London exhibition in due course.

It is very much hoped that a working relationship such as this, which has begun so well, based on an ever increasing and interactive vision of the dissemination of culture, will now go from strength to strength – for surely it is highly propitious that it should have come about because of Lorenzo il Magnifico, one of the few men who can truly be said to have had a hand in the fate of Europe.

Many thanks are due to all those who, both on their own behalf and on behalf of the cultural Institutions, have helped to make the exhibition and catalogue possible. The enthusiastic conviction of Rosa Maria Letts, the Chairman of the Accademia in London, was a major contributing factor as was the active interest of the Ministero degli Affari Esteri, thanks to the then Under Secretary, the On. Valdo Spini and to Elisabetta Kelescian's unstinting efforts. The support of the Committee for the Celebrations in Honour of the Fifth Centenary of the Death of Lorenzo il Magnifico ever since the idea of the exhibition was first mooted has been most welcome. Naturally none of this would have been possible without the generosity of the lenders (and of the libraries in particular) and the curators of the Florentine exhibitions who have patiently and competently advised me and helped with the choice of exhibits. Many of them have also contributed significantly to the catalogue. The Soprintendenza worked very closely with the Ufficio Centrale per i Beni Archeologici Ambientali Architettonici Artistici e Storici. As always, the Soprintendenza's Museum Directors and the officials who oversee the area have been generous with their time and effort, while Soprintendente Antonio Paolucci contributed an enormous amount of authoritative and friendly help. I should especially like to thank the Segreteria – Alberto Sassu, Marco Fossi and Cristina Gabbrielli in particular, assisted by Luciana Pasquini – without whose assiduous and dedicated work everything would have been in vain. Maria Sframeli's thoughtfulness and competence have been indispensible. Thanks are due to Lisa Venturini for helpful discussions. Last but not least, Roberta Cremoncini at the Accademia in London, who has been a tower of strength.

Cristina Acidini Luchinat
Soprintendente Vicario per i Beni Artistici e Storici di Firenze

Table of Contents

Fifteenth Century Florence

Florence, the Medici, the Territory
Francesca Klein

As an introduction to the reflection on Florentine civilization during the age of Lorenzo il Magnifico, the selection of documents from the Archivio di Stato is intended to pinpoint the most significant events and greatest themes of Laurentian politics. There are some important original works, some as yet unpublished and others that may provide the key to the literature of the time, possibly overturning established conceptions. This essay is an inevitably condenzed overview of the *Consorterie politiche e mutamenti istituzionali in età laurenziana* exhibition held in Spring/ Summer 1992, organised by the Archivio di Stato di Firenze together with the Sovrintendenza Archivistica per la Toscana and the Deputazione di Storia Patria per la Toscana.

The rise to power of the Medici family in Florence during the first Renaissance coincided with a period of important political and social change. At the beginning of the 15th century, the city was no longer the great mercantile and manufacturing centre (one of the most highly populated in the West, with over 100,000 inhabitants) that it had been only a century before, when it had been primarily concerned with safeguarding its own long-distance trading. 15th century Florence, in spite of the heavy demographic and economic losses it suffered as a result of recurrent serious crises, had managed to establish itself as the most important city in a territorial state, thanks to its bold expansionist policies, marking out for itself a prominent position amongst the powers on the Italian peninsula. The roots of the Medici hegemony in city life were planted, notoriously, on solid economic bases, thanks to the success of the family in banking matters. Cosimo de' Medici, Lorenzo's grandfather, was the first to trade his own mercantile fortune for testability of high office within the Florentine ruling classes. In 1434, at the head of a faction composed of representatives from a wide range of social milieux, he managed to topple the rival party then governing the State, thus bringing a political regime to an end. Not without uncertainties and contrasts, lacerations and bloodshed, the Medici rise to power changed the constitutional face of the Florentine Republic, creating a restricted State in which a few leading citizens were at the helm of the city.

That Cosimo's son, Piero, was aware of his own managerial vocation can be seen in the register of "remembrances" exhibited here. It was started on the death of Cosimo il Vecchio (1464), and intended as a record of the major milestones for what was rapidly becoming a political dynasty. The birth of the heir, Lorenzo, on 1st January 1449 was registered: "Lorenzo son of Piero, the elder, born in the year 1448 (according to Florentine custom) on the first day of January at 15 hours". The catch on the cover of the register bears

Cosimo's emblem of the diamond ring, symbolizing perpetuity, which was subsequently adopted by Piero. The Medici were already recognized as being Florence's premier family by the time Lorenzo first appeared on the political scene. The honour bestowed on Piero de' Medici and his heirs in perpetuity by Louis XI in 1465 in the right to add the fleur-de-lys to the Medici coat of arms, is the first mark of the Medici's elevation from the ranks of the working class they had once belonged to. Their ennoblement was a token of the great esteem in which the family was held. Until then their family crest had been decorated with simple balls or "palle" (not an uncommon emblem in Florentine heraldry), but as from 1465 they became entitled to add the three gold lilies on an azure background to the ball thereafter known as the "palla di Francia".

Piero de' Medici's short term of power was marked by great ructions within the Medici ranks, and he badly needed the young Lorenzo's support. In the city, Luca di Buonaccorso Pitti was organizing the anti-Medici movement, while Lorenzo, just sixteen, was being called to take his place on the committee charged with choosing citizens worthy of carrying out public duties. Cosimo had introduced a political system of intervention in electoral procedures, which traditionally took in Florence the form of drawing lots for public officials. A very tight control was maintained on political recruitment by the Ufficio delle Tratte and the unsupervised electoral committees of citizens. Between December 1465 and February 1466, both Lorenzo and his brother Giuliano qualified as Gonfaloniers of Justice. This involved a procedure in which selected names were placed in special ballot purses and then chosen by lot to assume the State's highest honour. On 2nd September 1466 Lorenzo, armed and on horseback, presided over the parliamentary session that restored power to the Medici "pro bono reipublice et pro pacifico statu civitatis Florentie".

It was particularly during the period immediately following his father's death (on 2nd December 1469) and after the institutional reforms of July 1471 that Lorenzo became recognized, albeit unofficially, as the first citizen of Florence. The dignity newly accorded to the Medici and to Lorenzo's own family in particular, no longer 'first among equals' but virtually the ruling family, is confirmed by numerous documents. One of these bears witness to the privilege which Ambrogio da Cora, General of the Agostiniani bestowed on Lorenzo and his family in recognition of their support during his own election to the generalship: the right to spiritual favours and affiliation to the Order, the elaborate illustrated inscription on the document bearing witness to the great esteem in which Lorenzo was held.

As early as 1472, Ser Simone Grazzini, trusted Notary to the Medici, wanted to institute a system completely new to Florentine legal practice – a register destined to record the hierarchy of Lorenzo's family, its assets and the honours awarded to it, such as, for example, the documents relative to the cardinalate of Lorenzo's son Giovanni, later to become Pope Leo X: "contractus et mandata et negocia et notas rerum gestarum per Magnificum Laurentium Petri Cosme de Medicis de Florentia". Grazzini became Segretario delle Tratte, the official who presided over electoral matters, in 1483. After Grazzini's death, his protocol book in its metal box was lodged with the secret Medici archives, being one of the fundamental documents relative to the Medici's princely rights.

Lorenzo's authority was backed up by a solid group of citizens, each of whom was bound by ties of fidelity to the Medici family and who constituted a well-bred government: these were the optimate Florentines who described themselves thus "nobilitate, prudentia et ingenio singulares, atque gubernande reipublice non mediocri scientia usuque prediti". In 1480 a constitutional move favoured by Lorenzo created the new Council of Seventy, which accorded a senatorial role to the optimates, who had automatic right of entry. The Council of Seventy were responsible for electing the Signoria, scrutinizing candidates for high office, such as the ambassadors and commissioners, the Dieci di Balia and the Otto di Guardia e Balia. They were also responsible for examining and discussing bills before they were passed to other citizens' committees. Document at p. 28 shows Chancellor Bartolomeo Scala, a reform ideologist, referring to the "Septuaginta viri", defining them as the "Florentinus Senatus": "quod senatorum officium fuit id vobis modo demandatum est et consiliis vestris, vestraque auctoritate et sententia universa respublica administranda est".

Within the district itself the patronal and business affairs of the Medici, and Lorenzo in particular, served to consolidate the Florentine territorial state, connecting its subjects ever more closely with the dominating power. These affairs were also one of the strongest elements in the weilding of Medici power through their control of Florentine politics throughout the territory. Lorenzo's determined and ill-advised attempted sacking of Volterra (1471-1472) is an illuminating example of this. The new terms imposed on the city by Florence are set out in the *Liber rerum Volaterranarum* and called for the total subjection of Volterra, her district and the surrounding area. Those Volterrans who had remained pro-Florentine and true to the Medici during the whole unpleasant episode were rewarded by being promoted to important city magistracies as a measure of Lorenzo's goodwill.

The Pazzi conspiracy was the event that really threatened both the internal and external political situation under Lorenzo. The well-known "infamous incident" which resulted in Lorenzo being wounded and Giuliano being killed during Mass in the church of Santa Reparata on 26th April 1478 triggered the war between Florence and Pope Sixtus IV, who was in league with the King of Naples. In order to deal with the dramatic situation within the city, Lorenzo initially joined the Otto di Guardia e Balia – the magistracy in charge of keeping order – but resigned on 18th May so as to avoid being accused of making use of his position to rid himself of his political enemies. The Otto, whose brief had already been greatly amplified with regard to the prevention and suppression of crimes and of political offences in particular, issued the *lex Gismondina* (named after Gismondo della Stufa, one of their number). This set of laws gave the Otto a more precise legislative brief and ensured that it was the highest-ranking penal magistrature of the State. The document exhibited here is the second draft of the law, dated 18th November 1478, and is the only existing copy. The first letter is illuminated to represent the allegory of Justice: by solemnly adhering to the principle of impartiality, the Otto were accorded exceptional powers including the right to inflict capital punishment and the right not to have to justify the punishments they meted out.

Lorenzo assumed without question that he could rely on the allegiance of foreign potentates, thanks to a network of diplomatic relations, and he regarded this as proof of his personal power. The success of his diplomatic mission to Naples culminated on 13th March 1480 in the signing of peace and alliance with the major Italian powers (the Papacy, the Kingdom of Naples, Milan, Florence and Siena), resulting a *détente* between Florence, Sixtus IV and Ferdinand of Aragon. On 19th December 1479, Lorenzo had arrived in Naples, having decided to travel without diplomatic papers, to negotiate peace as head of State rather than as representative citizen ("suo proprio et privato nomine"). He managed to reaffirm the principles of "political equilibrium" based, as has been observed, on the Triple Alliance with Naples and Milan, which accorded Florence and its renowned leader the role of central mediator over the whole Italian political scene.

Lorenzo il Magnifico died on 8th April 1492 and the whole city went into mourning for their "Signore", as he is referred to in the note in the Priorista delle Riformagioni. This was the register in which the names of the Priors and Gonfaloniers of Justice were recorded as they took up office. The Priorista, which is now kept in the archives of the Palazzo della Signoria, was available for consultation and as an article of public faith, but during the 15th century it also became an instrument for political propaganda because of the details of local events it contained. To a certain extent, as Machiavelli pointed out, Lorenzo's death coincided with the end of an era: quite soon "those evil seeds began to sprout, and in the absence of he who knew how to eradicate them, they soon began to poison Italy and indeed continue to do so". In the difficult days that followed, Lorenzo's funeral was censured by Savonarola's anti-Medici government, and the entry in the appropriate register heavily scored out (traces of the original handwriting can now only be detected by ultraviolet light) with long oblique strokes that reveal just how all-consuming was the rage and the violence with which they wished to eradicate his memory. The record that can be seen today is of a later date, and was probably made during the time of political and documentary Medici restoration.

Well into the 16th century, the Cafaggiolo branch of the Medici finally took up Lorenzo il Magnifico's legacy and under Cosimo I overcame the glorious Republican institutes, finally establishing the Principality.

Selected Bibliography

Statuta Populi et Communis Florentiae, publica auctoritate collecta, castigata et praeposita anno salutis MCCCCXV, Friburgi apud Kluch (but Florence, Cambiagi), 1778-1783.

A. Fabroni: *Laurentii Medicis vita*, Pisis 1791-1795.

F. Rinuccini: *Ricordi storici dal 1282 al 1460 colla continuazione di Alamanno e Neri Rinuccini suoi figli fino al 1506*, G. Aiazzi (ed.), Florence 1840.

A.H. Sarzanensis: *Historia de volaterrana calamitate*, F.L. Mannucci (ed.), Città di Castello 1913.

Statuti della Repubblica fiorentina, ed. by Comune di Firenze da Romolo Caggese, I, *Statuti del Capitano del Popolo degli anni 1322-1325*, Florence 1910; II, *Statuti del Podestà dell'anno 1325*, Florence 1917-1921.

E. Fiumi: *L'impresa di Lorenzo de' Medici contro Volterra (1472)*, Florence 1948.

Protocolli del carteggio di Lorenzo il Magnifico per gli anni 1473-74, 1477-92, M. Del Piazzo (ed.), Florence 1956.

R. De Roover: *The Rise and Decline of the Medici Bank, 1397-1494*, Cambridge (Mass.) 1963.

N. Rubinstein: *The Government of Florence under the Medici 1434 to 1494)*, Oxford 1966.

D. Kent: *The rise of Medici faction in Florence*, Oxford 1978.

G. Chittolini: *La formazione dello stato regionale e le istituzioni del contado, secoli XIV-XV*, Turin 1979.

R. Fubini: *Appunti sui rapporti diplomatici sul dominio sforzesco e Firenze medicea*, in *Gli Sforza a Milano e in Lombardia e i loro rapporti con gli stati italiani ed europei (1450-1530)*, Milan 1982.

R. Fubini: *Federico da Montefeltro e la congiura dei Pazzi: politica e propaganda alla luce di nuovi documenti*, in *Federico di Montefeltro. Lo stato*, G. Cerboni Baiardi, G. Chittolini and P. Floriani (ed.), Rome 1986.

R. Fubini: *Classe dirigente ed esercizio della diplomazia nella Firenze quattrocentesca*, in *I ceti dirigenti nella Toscana del Quttrocento*, Monte Oriolo 1987.

D. Marzi: *La Cancelleria della Repubblica Fiorentina*, Rocca San Casciano 1910; rep. Florence 1987.

A. Zorzi: *L'amministrazione della giustizia penale nella Repubblica fiorentina. Aspetti e problemi*, Florence 1988.

Archivio delle Tratte, P. Viti, R.M. Zaccaria (ed.), Rome 1989.

R. Fubini: *L'età delle congiure; i rapporti tra Firenze e Milano dal tempo di Piero a quello di Lorenzo de' Medici (1464-1478)* in *Florence and Milan: comparisions and relations, Acts of two conferences at Villa I Tatti in 1982-1984*, II, Florence 1989.

Lorenzo dei Medici: *Lettere*, voll. I-II, R. Fubini (ed.), Florence 1977; voll. III-IV, N. Rubinstein (ed.), Florence 1977-1981; voll. V-VI, M. Mallet (ed.), Florence 1989-1990.

A. Brown: *Bartolomeo Scala, 1430-1497, Chancellor of Florence, the Humanist as Bureaucrat*, Princeton 1979.

R. Fubini: 'Dalla rappresentanza sociale alla rappresentanza politica: alcune osservazioni sull'evoluzione politico-costituzionale di Firenze nel Rinascimento', in *Rivista Storica Italiana*, CII (1990).

R. Fubini: 'Cultura umanistica e tradizione cittadina nella storiografia fiorentina del '400, in *Atti e memorie dell'Accademia Toscana di Scienze e lettere 'La Colombaria'*, LVI (1991).

M.A. Timpanaro Morelli, R. Mano Tolu, P. Viti (ed.), *Consorterie politiche e mutamenti istituzionali in età laureanziana*, (Florence), Milan 1992.

Niccolò Valori's *Vita di Lorenzo* in Various Manuscripts and Editions
Paola Pirolo

Recent research has identified Valori's biography as being one of the greatest sylloges of the tributes paid to Lorenzo between the fifteenth and sixteenth centuries, second only to Redditi's *Exortatio ad Petrum Medicem in magnanimi parentis imitationem*, on which Valori's work draws to a certain extent. This connection apart, however, it should also be stressed that there is a considerable difference between the contemporary interpretation of events contained in the *Exortatio* and the altogether more thematic approach of Valori's *Vita*, and this in spite of a certain mutuality... Redditi's sylloge presents the myth of Lorenzo in a quite markedly different way not only to the severe condemnations (following the tragic failure of the Pazzi conspiracy) in Alamanno Rinuccini's *De libertate*, but also to Francesco Rinuccini's criticisms of Lorenzo and his accolytes in the *Ricordi* immediately after the statesman's death, not to mention the denunciation of Lorenzo's insatiable thirst for domination and his arbitrary liberties in fiscal and economic matters contained in Cambi's *Istorie*. The evaluation of these differences, together with particular assonances between the *Vita* and the *Exortatio* depends not so much on the content, which in both cases is openly encomiastic, but on the different political ideological contexts of both books, particularly in the different significance that the *Vita* assumes in each of its versions and in subsequent editions: 1494-98, 1513, 1517-21, 1567 and 1568. The *Exortatio* was written between late 1487 and early 1489 and bears the unmistakable traces of Redditi's devotion to the Medici party and of his univocal political activism, describing the Laurentian regime and its end quite accurately, though in a wholly approving manner.

The *Vita* is quite a different matter, and so in general terms were the three generations of the Valori family (Niccolò, Filippo and Baccio) each of whom contributed to a greater or larger extent to its elaboration. The Valori family were closely involved in the dramatic events under all the political regimes spanning 1494-98 (a period which saw the ostracising of Piero de' Medici, Savonarola's rapid rise and subsequent fall, and the invasion of Charles VIII, King of France), until the princedom of Cosimo I (from 9th January 1537 until August 1569).

This was a period studded with events that caused the three generations of the Valori family to have to adapt to the Medici restoration of 1512 (after the fall of Soderini's Gonfalonierato) and then to the successive happenings under Popes Leo X (1513-1521) and Clement VII (1523), including an interval (between 1527-30) when the Medici were again expelled, the progressive consolidation of an absolutist regime under Alessandro de' Medici (created head of the Florentine Republic by Carlo V, then assassinated on 6th January 1537) particularly under Cosimo I.

The *Vita* could well, therefore, have been the means by which Niccolò, Filippo and Baccio Valori attempted to survive what was for them a very unfavourable political alliance, paying tribute to Lorenzo not for his own sake, nor as a simple act of submission to the Medici family, but playing on it as a means of reaffirming the role the Valori family were to occupy during the Laurentian era – a role subsequently compromised by Piero's incapacities, which had to a certain extent, justified Republican approaches. The Valori "myth" was therefore at the real heart of the *Vita*, and the defence of Lorenzo was the necessary vehicle for an attempt at survival that was not to be exhausted by requests for pardons through obsequiousness towards that dynasty from which Lorenzo's work has deservedly been singled out for celebration, rather than that of his successors.

The affinities between the *Vita*, Guicciardini's *Elogio di Lorenzo de' Medici* and Machiavelli's portrait of Lorenzo contained in the final volume of the *Istorie Fiorentine* have long been recognized, and there exists between them a relationship that remains hard to define in relation to a chronology that remains controversial. In fact, although there are undoubted similarities, proving that there is indeed a relationship between the three, and a common preoccupation with their alignment with the "post 1512" political scene, there appears to be no question of a univocal mutualisation either by Valori, nor by Guicciardini in his *Elogio* (which is a unique Guicciardini portrait leading directly back to the *Vita*), nor indeed by Machiavelli.

The partial convergence (which partly explains the passages common to both, which are in fact strenuously emphasized) of Guicciardini and Valori's writing on questions of adhesion to the regime of Medici restoration has revealed a perceptible ideological shift both in the *Elogio* (as compared with the much more criticized *Storie Fiorentine*) and in the *Vita* (as compared with Valori's own *Ricordanze*). Defining the quality of Valori's ideological forcing is hugely important as regards the real meaning behind his *revirement*, for one simple act of submission can be interpreted in several different ways. Here there is the intentional reproposition of the old 'Valoria Domus' and 'Domus Medica' alliance in accordance with Ficino's doctrine.

Lorenzo's religiosity goes right back to his childhood. "Affermava esso M. gentile col quale vissi sempre in grandissima familiarità, & massime nella sua legazione al Christianissimo Re di Francia, che non mai Lorenzo si partiva da lui, segno in uno giovanetto di intera modestia, il giorno in mentre che si celebrava sempre seco ne templi, la notte di più voleva seguitare la compagnia di San Pagolo, dove molti convengono intenti a sobrietà, vigilie & orazioni accompagnando egli le preci con abbondantissime limosine, né in quella tenera età mai essersi mostra voglia puerile, o desiderio superfluo, per lo che non essere da maravigliarsi se per divino favore fu di poi a tanta degnità inalzato, o che la Italia fusse quieta & tranquilla vivente lui, & dopo la morte sua tutta confusa & perturbata, come se la salute di lei in la vita di Lorenzo consistesse" (Valori, *Vita del Mag. Lorenzo de' Medici il Vecchio…*, Florence 1568, c. a2v). This theme is reverted to immediately afterwards, in terms of Lorenzo's influence on pontifical matters. After an initial favour granted by Sixtus IV (who handed over the finances of the Curia to Lorenzo, causing Giovanni Tornabuoni, his maternal uncle, to become suddenly rich through his handling of the sale of the treasures amassed by Paul III), the loss of his support as a result of the Pazzi conspiracy was tempered by the fact that God seemed to smile on him in adversity (adversity intended, as with Machiavelli, to prove his virtue).

Lorenzo always seemed to trust in divine providence, such as when he was about to set out on the dangerous journey to Naples. The effect of his 'religiosity' is taken up towards the end of the *Vita* where there is a clear differentiation between 'neoplatonism' and 'christianity'.

In 1749, on the occasion of the first impression of the Latin version, one hundred and eighty years after the first Italian edition of Niccolò Valori's *Vita* (in 1568, Giunti typ.) was printed, Lorenzo Mehus (or Meo) declared that the Italian version was not, as had always been thought, the work of Niccolò (rather his son Filippo) and that the Laur. Plut. LXI,3 manuscript (M. Martelli, 'Le due redazioni della Laurenti Medicei vita', *Bibliofilia*, LXVI, 1964, p. 242) was the original one. In all probability this version was likely simply to have been a later Latin edition of an earlier (circa 1494) draft, now lost. Nonetheless it was from this version that Mehus drew up the 1749 edition, using the same letter of dedication from Niccolò to Leo X. Here Valori claims to have written the *Vita* immediately after Lorenzo's death, that he was reluctant to publish it because he feared his style was not good enough for the subject matter and that only then (at a date traceable to De' Rossi's cardinalate i. e. between 1517-1521, De' Rossi having quite clearly been behind the initiative), having revised it advisedly, he decided to dedicate it to him as a symbol of their mutual devotion to Lorenzo.

Abbot Lorenzo Mehus – one of the top philologers of the 18th century, Prefect of the Biblioteca Medicea Laurenziana, Member of the Accademia Etrusca di Cortona and correspondent of most of the great European intellectuals – edited Bruni and Salutati's letters (1741) and Fazio's *De viris illustribus* (1745), Salutati's *De discordiis Florentinorum* (1747), and Manetti's *Specimen historiae litterariae Florentinae* (1747). He published the Latin version of Valori's *Vita* in 1749, and Traversari's *Epistole* in 1759 (G. Natali, *Il settecento*, Milan, Vallardi, 1960, vol. I, pp. 425-426).

By dedicating the *Vita* to Baron Firmian, Mehus establishes a parallel between the nobleman from Trent and Lorenzo, united by their political prestige and their patronage of the Arts. Carlo Firmian, the Austrian Minister in Lombardy was well known for his protection and encouragement of philosophical, literary and scientific pursuits.

He was a promoter of political reform and was responsible for the growth of both public and private libraries. This comparison between Firmian and Lorenzo underlines the now well-established third type of *posthumous image* of Lorenzo: that of the prince of letters and patrons. "… Si quis autem in medium adducat LAURENTII MEDICEI sedulitatem in perquirendis Veterum monumentis, Codicibusque ex barbarorum manibus eripiendis, quibus celeberrimam Mediceam Bibliothecam Matthiae Corvini Hungariae Regis exemplo excitaret, ac spoliis Orientis ab Ioanne Lascare Florentiam deportandis locupletaret; is non inficiabitur, TE quoque hanc LAURENTII curam aemulari…" (L. Mehus, [Dedicatoria], in: N. Valori, *Vita*, cit. p. VII). The spread of the Laurentian myth codified by Valori in the 18th century owed much to Goujet's translation (cf. N. Valori, *La vie de Laurent de Médicis, surnommé le Grand et Père des lettres, Chef de la République de Florence; addressée au Pape Léon X: traduit du latin… avec des notes, & quelques Pièces anciennes qui ont rapport au même sujet, à Paris,* chez Nyon, 1761, 16°) published with Notes, and the French versions of several significant documents (Giacomo Antiquario's letter to Poliziano and the latter's reply, on the subject of Lorenzo's death; Redditi's *Exortatio*). In the preface to this *Vie de Laurent de Médicis…*, Abbot Claude Pierre Goujet (indefatigable writer, author of weighty volumes of ecclesiastical history, responsible for the additions and corrections to Moreri's *Dictionnaire* and compiler of the *Bibliothèque Française* and contributor to the *Journal des Savans*) describes the evolution of the work, from the first draft to Mehus' Latin edition, taking care to emphasize that his own translation derives from the latter. Although the Abbot remains perplexed by the existence of two different Latin versions of the work, on the other hand he has managed to grasp perfectly the continuous eulogistic line that links Redditi's sylloge to Valori's, only to become disembowelled in Jove, Boissat and Varillas's formalised canonizations of Lorenzo's image. "L'Eloge composé par Paul Jove, n'apprend aucun fait; ... ce que dit Boissat est encore plus superficiel: à l'égard de Varillas, son Histoire est melée d'anecdotes supposées, & d'Avantures Romanesques..." (cf. C. P. Goujet, *Préface* a N. Valori, *La vie*, cit, pp. XXIII-XXIV).

Selected Bibliography

E. Garin: *Giovanni Pico della Mirandola, Vita e dottrina*, Florence, Le Monnier, 1937.

F. Gilbert: 'Guicciardini, Machiavelli, Valori on Lorenzo il Magnifico', *Renaissance News*, XI n. 2 (Summer 1958) pp. 107-114.

E. Garin: *Medioevo e Rinascimento. Studi e richerche*, Bari, Laterza, 1961.

E. Garin: *La cultura filosofica del Rinascimento Italiano*, Florence, Sansoni, 1961.

M. Martelli: 'Le due redazioni della Laurentii Medicei Vita di Niccolò Valori', *Bibliofilia*, LXVI, 1964, pp. 234-253.

F. Gilbert: *Machiavelli e Guicciardini. Pensiero politico e storiografia a Firenze nel Cinquecento*, Turin, Einaudi, 1970.

F. Gilbert: *Machiavelli e il suo tempo*, Bologna, Il Mulino, 1977.

E. Gusberti: 'Un mito del Cinquecento: Lorenzo il Magnifico', *Bollettino dell'Istituto storico italiano per il Medio evo. Archivio Muratoriano*, 91 (1984), pp. 183-279.

N. Rubinstein: *The formation of the posthumous Image of Lorenzo de' Medici*, in Plures, *Oxford, China and Italy. Writing in Honour of Sir Harold Acton on his Eightieth Birthday*, ed. E. Chaney and N. Ritchie, London, Thames & Hudson, 1984.

C. M. Kovesi: 'Niccolò Valori and the Medici restoration of 1512. Politics, eulogies and the preservation of a family myth'. *Rinascimento*, S. II, XXVII, 1987, pp. 301-325.

F. Redditi: '*Exortatio ad Petrum Medicem*,' *con appendice di lettere*. Introduction, critical text and comments by P. Viti, Florence, Olschki, 1988.

The Medici and the City

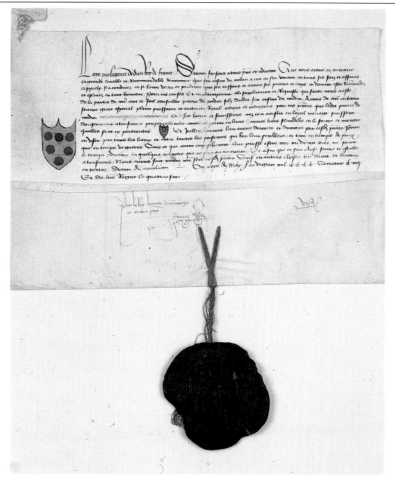

Louis XI, King of France, Authorizes Piero de' Medici and His Heirs and Successors to Add the French Armorial Bearings to the Medici Coat of Arms
Parchment; 352 x 343 mm; pendant seal, hanging from document by cord; circular impression in green wax (102 mm diameter)
Archivio di Stato di Firenze, Diplomatico, Mediceo, May 1465

Memoirs of Piero di Cosimo: Recollection of Lorenzo's Birth 1464
Paper ledger; 365 x 250 mm; 222 leaves, contemporary numbering; black leather stamped binding with clasp
Archivio di Stato di Firenze, Mediceo avanti il Principato 163
(Work without illustration)

The Qualification of Lorenzo and Giuliano de' Medici to Gonfaloniership of Justice in 1465-66
Paper, loose leaf; 296 x 220 mm; 8 leaves; modern pencilled numbering, top right margin. The same margin shows 18th-century numbering referring to a series of miscellaneous documents which these leaves formed part of
Archivio di Stato di Firenze, Tratte 398

"Protocol Record [...]: Contracts of Simone Grazzini Pertaining to the Medici Household"
17th August 1472-12th May 1494
Paper ledger; 325 x 240 mm; contemporary numbering; parchment binding; this also has a preliminary inventory, handwritten shortly afterwards (attributable to Tommaso di Matteo Grazzini), 34 leaves, contemporary numbering and a separate 16th-century inventory, on paper, 40 leaves, contemporary numbering; parchment binding. The two ledgers (protocol and inventory) are kept in a hinged tin box, 330 x 260 x 115 mm
Archivio di Stato di Firenze, Notarile Antecosimiano 10200

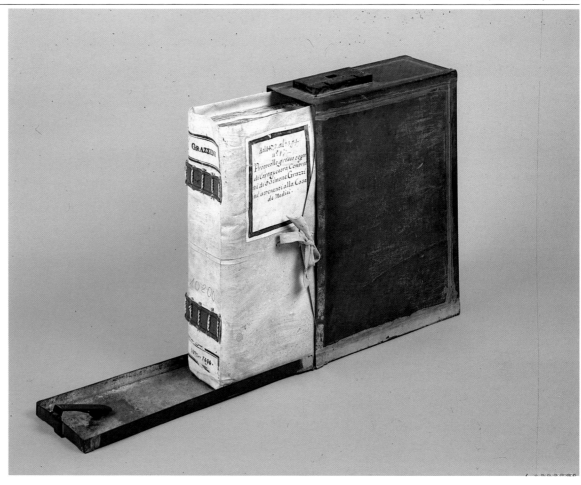

General of the Order of the Augustinians, Ambrogio da Cori, Confers Membership to the Order, and the Right to Spiritual Benefits, to Lorenzo de' Medici and Family
Florence, February 1st 1477
Parchment; initial 'LAURENTIO' illuminated with Medici coat of arms; 253 x 488 mm
Archivio di Stato di Firenze, Diplomatico, Mediceo, 1477 February 1st

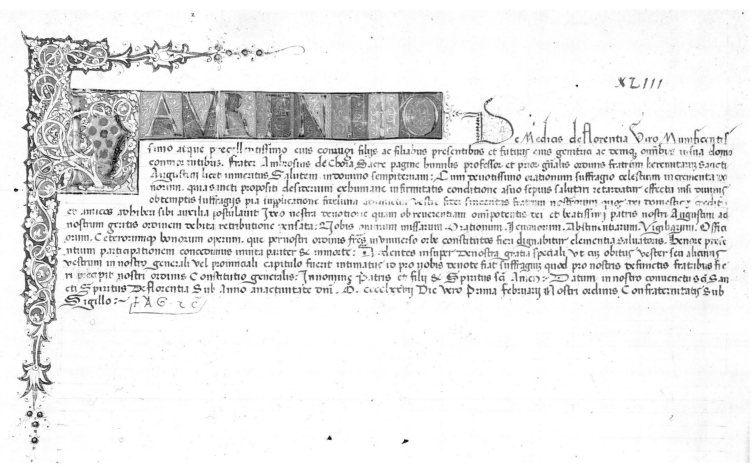

Deliberations of the "Consiglio dei Settanta"
19th April 1480
Parchment booklet; 320 x 235 mm;
10 leaves numbered at a later date
(leaves 40-49), unbound
Archivio di Stato di Firenze,
Miscellanea Repubblicana 4, 115

NON sine magna causa institutu est iurare in Leges Magistratus, et omnes fere qui
publicae alicui administrationi sunt prefuturi. Reges etiam no nisi quibusdam prius
uncti atq initiati sacris regnu ineunt. Unde et christos prisci nominauerunt idest
unctos: Quanq unus est uere christus et Rex noster filius dei: Nos quoq comuni
quadam et uulgata appellatione sacros Reges diamus: eorumq Maiestatem excellenti
huiusmodi cognomento saepissime honestamus. Principi enim illi rex omnium Deo
qui fecit hominem ad ymaginem et similitudinem suam cure certe est genus humanu:
Quod quidem comodissime seruatur atq excolitur his coetibus que appellantur Ciuitates
atq his magistratibz quibus huiusmodi hominu societates et consortia recte administrant.
Merito igitur sacre dicuntur leges sacra Iura: que ad hominu utilitatem et decus
sunt constituta: eorum etiam auctores caelo sepe donauit Antiquitas. Cum haec
ita sint quid conuenientius q in Leges iurare eos qui publicas sunt personas accepturi
et prefuturi humanis coetibus. Vos quoq septuaginta uiri nobile concilium quas gem
tis personas etiam atq etiam consideretis oportet et munus uestru intelligatis: In omni
ciuitate quedam publica sunt: quedam priuata et priuatis quidem quisq pro arbitrio
inseruit: publica aliam ratione habent. Primu enim ut sint qui ea curent multo
etiam q priuata diligentius necesse est. Deinde quibus id muneris contigit: ut in ea
ratione meminerint Ciuitatis obliuiscantur sui. Quanq si recte ratiocinari quis
uelit: Intelliget in bono publico contineri suu: neq aduersari publica comoda priua
tis. Vos autem ij estis septuaginta uiri: quibus modo et salutem patria credidit
et dignitatem: Curare uos omni studio oportet: ut eam tanti in uos collati honoris
nunq poeniteat. Romani uestri generis auctores huic muneri prefectos appellauerut
patres similitudine cure. Vos ergo patria uestra estis patres quo nihil neq dici
neq excogitari potest honoratius. Hic enim est Florentinus Senatus: si ut Liuius
scribit Senatus est uniuscuiusq ciuitatis publicu Consilium. Mira fuit

The Lex Gismondina, "Orders of the 'Otto di guardia e balia' (the eight civic guardians) of Florence"
18th November 1478
Parchment ledger; 250 x 220 mm; numbered at a later date; bound in crimson velvet with metallic corner decorations, protective supports and decorative panels, one containing the Medici coat of arms, the other a knight
Archivio di Stato di Firenze, Otto di guardia e di balia, Repubblica 226

D 1ᵉ · XV · iulij · In consilio del cento |

OLATERANA VRBE SITV NATVRAQ͜ MVNI=
tissima, fauente altissimo / in ius potestatemq͜ florentini ppłi
breui redacta : quod nunq͜ apud alios italie populos credunt̃ ē
et nostre ... ciuitat... difficillimum factu ēt : Primum qdem
summo deo immortales agende gratie sunt pro tam ingenti
etiam optato beneficio : deinde ita procurandum ēt : ut quod summis laboribus
magnisq͜ uigiliis & anxietatibus : atq͜ ingentibus sumptibus licet summo cū honore
partum ēt : perpetuo nobis construetur : indq͜ illud omni studio cura opera et
diligentia incumbendum : Precipue cum sit pluribus et uariis ediuersis rebus et
magni ponderis prouidendum : in quibus iustitia in regendo · clementia in uictos
prouidentia in disponendo · securitas in custodiendo adhiberi debet : cuimq͜ ad nichil
ac maturius p grauissimos auctoritate eprudentia uiros fieri q͜ aliter possit :
Jotiro magnifici e excelsi domini · D · P · L · et vexi iustitie populi florẽ : ut ǧto

"Liber rerum volaterranarum"
30th April 1472-28th June 1514
Parchment ledger; 420 x 320 mm;
I-IV, 160; contemporary numbering;
with inventory; bound in board
and leather
Archivio di Stato di Firenze,
Capitoli 61

**Letter of Lorenzo il Magnifico
to Girolamo Morelli in Milan**
Florence, 22nd-23rd June 1478
Paper; 295 x 220 mm; original
Archivio di Stato di Firenze,
Mediceo avanti il Principato,
XCVI, 74
(Work without illustration)

**Treaty Drafted in Naples on 13th
March 1480**
Parchment book; 345 x 246 mm;
16 leaves, not numbered
Archivio di Stato di Firenze,
Diplomatico (a quaderno),
1480 March 13th

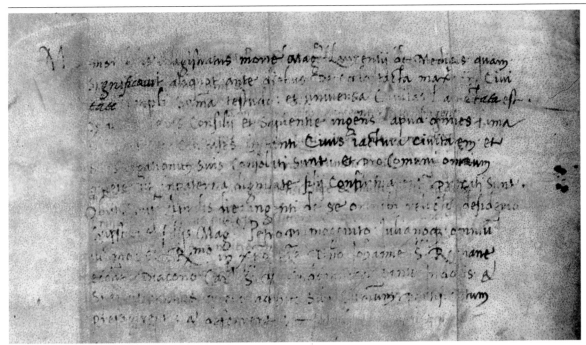

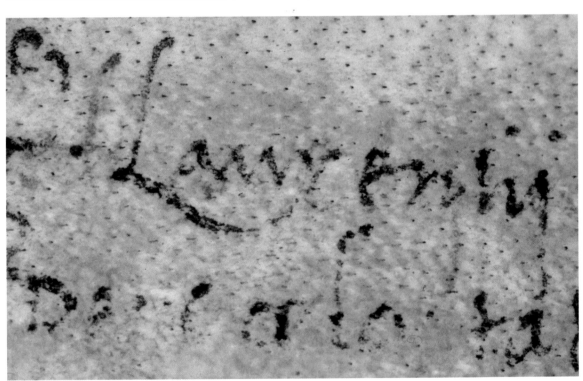

Roll of Priors of the "Riformagioni" Containing Notes on the Death of Lorenzo, Censored during Savonarola's Rule
12th June 1282-30th April 1532
Parchment ledger; 410 x 270 mm;
II, 348; contemporary numbering;
binding in red leather covered board
with metallic corner trims cut into
floral shapes
Archivio di Stato di Firenze,
Tratte 57

Florentine Culture

Seal of Florence (17th-18th century)
Steel; 26 mm diameter
Florence, Museo Nazionale
del Bargello (Inv. no. 1426)

Seal of Luca degli Albizi
(16th century)
Bronze; 37 mm diameter, 56 mm h.
Florence, Museo Nazionale
del Bargello (Inv. no. 12118)

Seal of the "Conservatori di Legge"
(custodians of the law) of Florence
Bronze; 45 mm diameter, 65 mm h.
Florence, Museo Nazionale
del Bargello (Inv. no. 509)

Seal of Maso degli Albizi
(1402-1417)
Bronze, 42 mm diameter
Florence, Museo Nazionale
del Bargello (Inv. no. 617)

Seal of Cardinal Giovanni Salviati
(1518-1521)
Bronze; 117 x 72 mm
Florence, Museo Nazionale
del Bargello (Inv. no. 1442)

Cosimo il Vecchio de' Medici
Florence, second half of the 15th
century
Bronze; 80 mm diameter
Florence, Museo Nazionale
del Bargello (Inv. no. 5993)

Lorenzo il Magnifico
Florence, 16th century
Silver; coin; 28.4 mm diameter
Florence, Museo Nazionale
del Bargello (Inv. no. 6041)

Marsilio Ficino
16th-century Florentine school
Bronze; 60 mm diameter, pierced
Florence, Museo Nazionale
del Bargello (Inv. no. 10222)

Pope Leo X
16th-century Roman school
Gold-plated bronze; 33.2 mm
diameter
Florence, Museo Nazionale
del Bargello (Inv. no. 7058)

Niccolò Fiorentino
Giovanni Pico della Mirandola
Bronze; 83.3 mm diameter
Florence, Museo Nazionale
del Bargello (Inv. no. 6001)

Fra Girolamo Savonarola
Florence, late 15th century
Lead; 30.5 x 41 mm
Florence, Museo Nazionale
del Bargello (Inv. no. 6024)

Lisippo the Younger
Pope Sixtus IV
Lead; 40.1 mm diameter
Florence, Museo Nazionale
del Bargello (Inv. no. 6104)

Gian Francesco Eurola
**Francesco I and Galeazzo di Milano,
Fourth and Fifth Dukes of Milan**
Brass, modern casting
45.6 mm diameter, pierced
Florence, Museo Nazionale
del Bargello (Inv. no. 5941)

Niccolò Fiorentino
Angelo Poliziano e Maria Poliziana
Bronze; 53.2 mm diameter
Florence, Museo Nazionale
del Bargello (Inv. no. 6002)

Jug, with Handle and Spout
Cafaggiolo c 1510-1520
Enamelled earthenware decorated
with Medici-Salviati crest
26 cm h.
Florence, Museo Nazionale
del Bargello (Inv. maioliche no. 120)

Jug
Cafaggiolo 1515
Enamelled earthenware with portrait
of Leo X
h. 35 cm, diameter 14.8 cm
Faenza, Museo Internazionale
delle Ceramiche
(Work without illustration)

The Life of Lorenzo the Magnificent

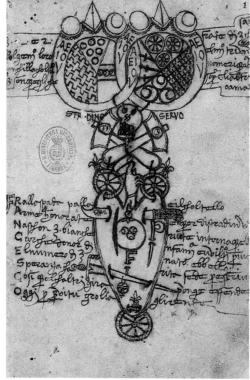

Niccolò Valori
**Vita del Magnifico Lorenzo
de' Medici tradotta da Filippo
suo figliuolo**
(The life of the Magnificent
Lorenzo dei Medici, translated
by Filippo Valori)
Florence, 16th century
Parchment; 225 x 150 mm; 62 leaves;
bound in board with leather spine
Gilt embossed edge
Biblioteca Nazionale Centrale
di Firenze, Panc. 172

Niccolò Valori
Vita di Lorenzo il Magnifico
(in miscellaneous manuscript)
Florence, mid-16th century
Paper; miscellaneous; 208 x 104 mm,
I°, machine numbered on outer top
margin. Half leather binding and
paper decorated with small seals;
spine divided in four parts by chains
stamped in gold: STRAD/STOR/MEDIC/
& C.
Biblioteca Riccardiana di Firenze,
2599

Niccolò Valori
**Vita di Lorenzo tradotta da Baccio
suo nipote e dedicata a Cosimo I**
(Life of Lorenzo, Translated by
Valori's Grandson Baccio and
Dedicated to Cosimo I)
Florence, 1567
Paper; 320 x 220 mm; I, 60, I°
Original Laurentian binding
Biblioteca Mediceo-Laurenziana
di Firenze, Plut. 61. 18

Niccolò Valori
**Vita / del Mag. Lorenzo /
De' Medici / Il Vecchio, / Scritta da
Niccolo Valori / Patritio Fiorentino. /
Nuovamente posta in luce. /
Con licenza & Privilegio**
(The life of the Magnificent Lorenzo
the Elder written by Niccolò Valori,
Florentine nobleman, printed, with
permission, by Giunti in 1568)
quarto (28), reg.: (*) 2 a-f4g2
Biblioteca Nazionale Centrale di
Firenze, Palat. C.2.3.54, 16 x 22.5 cm
(Work without illustration)

Biagio Buonaccorsi, Niccolò Valori
**Diario / de' successi più importanti /
Seguiti in Italia, & particolarmente /
in Fiorenza dall'anno 1498 in /
sino all'anno 1512 / Raccolto da Biagio
Buonaccorsi in que' tempi coadiu-/
tore in Segreteria de Magnifici
signori / Dieci della Guerra della
città / di Fiorenza / con la vita del
Magnifico Lorenzo / de' Medici il
Vecchio / Scritta da Niccolò Valori
Patrizio Fiorentino. / Nuovamente
posta in luce. / In Fiorenza /
Appresso i Giunti / 1568. / Con
licenza & Privilegio**
(Chronicle of the most important
events in Italy, and in particular in
Florence, from the year 1498 to the
year 1512, compiled by Biagio
Buonaccorsi, in that period
'Coadiutore in segreteria' to the
Signori Dieci della Guerra in the city
of Florence. With the Life of the
Magnificent Lorenzo de' Medici the
Elder. Written by Niccolò Valori,
Florentine nobleman, printed, with
permission, by Giunti in 1568)
quarto, p. (56) 184 (8), reg.: (*) 2
a-f4a2 A-AA4
Biblioteca Nazionale Centrale
di Firenze, Palat. C.1.4.12,
15.5 x 22.5 cm
(Work without illustration)

LAURENTII MEDICEI / Vita / a
Nicolao Valorio / scripta / ex cod.
Mediceo-Laurentiano / nunc
primum latine in lucem eruta /
cura, et studio / Laurentii mehus /
etruscae academiae cortonensis
socii. / Florentiae Anno mdccil /
**Ex Typographio I0. Pavlli
Giovannelli. / Praesidibus**
adprobantibus
1749
8° XV, 67 (ma 69) +8A-C8D12 (-D12)
Biblioteca Nazionale Centrale
di Firenze, Rinasc. Medici 81
(previously 7956.26), 21.5 x 13.5 cm

The Medicean Architecture: Buildings and Theories

Laurentian Architecture – An Outline
Gabriele Morolli

The traditional picture of 15th century Florence architectonically hegemonized by Brunelleschi and his followers, where from the first 'glorious' and 'revolutionary' twenty years up to the highly refined *fin de siècle* of the late Humanism of Lorenzo il Magnifico and his court artist, Giuliano da Sangallo, there had 'reigned' a uniform building vocabulary characterized by the informed use of classical frames in *pietra serena* covered with coats of render, designed with regard to the perspectival articulation of the city space, now appears frankly improbable in the light of closer historiographical inspection.

Just as in the sister fields of painting and sculpture there is a deep divide between Masaccio or Donatello's peremptory plastic solutions and the restless search of artists such as Leonardo, Verrocchio and Antonio del Pollaiolo who sought multiform and fleeting solutions, there is a great difference between Brunelleschi's aggressive and aurorean classicism and the precious antique philologism of architects such as Sangallo and his circle within the specific ambit of the *De Re Aedificatoria*.

Just as in politics (and particularly in cultural politics), Piero the Gouty with his shrewd architectonic commissions which anticipated a renewed demand for the rarer archaeological shapes such as affected combinations, heterodox Ionic orders, rather than the Neo-Romanesque traditionalistic Ionic and Corinthian styles, came between the pragmatic Cosimo de' Medici and the refined, decadent Lorenzo, the pivotal figure of Leon Battista Alberti, who can be regarded as the needle on the aesthetic scales of the entire century, came between Brunelleschi and Sangallo, who were at opposite extremes of architectonic Humanism. Alberti, who was a great theoretician as well as a very great architect, had been responsible for providing a whole generation of mid-15th century architects with new tools and perspectives which they could apply to the works of the venerated masters of old in an endeavour to capture the shapes which, duly transformed and developed, formed the basis for the new vocabulary of the 'Modern' architecture. This he achieved through his buildings (from the Palazzo Rucellai with its grid of superimposed pilasters to the marble tomb in the chapel of the church of San Pancrazio and the pedimented marble temple facade of the church of Santa Maria Novella, all for the Rucellai family and through his treatises (notably his *De Re Aedificatoria*, 'published' in 1452).

In attempting an examination of the reality of Florence's construction industry during the middle of the 15th century, other than in the light of the traditional historiography of the above-mentioned age-old hegemony of Brunelleschi's creations, one could frankly conclude that if on one hand Brunelleschi's great 'fossils' (from San Lorenzo to Santo Spirito to the Lantern of the Cupola of the Duomo, to the Pitti Palace) continued to be built unremittingly until the 1470s or 1480s, steadily losing momentum, on the other hand architectonic features, rich in aesthetic vitality, began to appear at the forefront of the construction debate. Take, for example, the marvellous marble monuments both in the church of Santissima Annunziata (a church with a significant very modern four-sided portico and a smaller two-column entrance) and in the church of San Miniato al Monte (patronized, not by chance, by Piero de' Medici) of the 1450s, the cryptically Albertian principles of the Badia Fiesolana (also patronized by Piero) and the portico of the Cappella dei Pazzi (not Brunelleschi's work but that of Rossellino) of the 1460s, and the Tribune of Santa Annunziata built by Alberti in 1470 as a circular *templum* with an antique cupola. There was also the equally innovative 'decorative architecture' of the fine marble fitments made by Rossellino and Desiderio, which was still full of Albertian references (viz the tombs of Leonardo Bruni and Carlo Marsuppini) and which found its own synthesis and monumental amplification in important chapels such as the Cardini chapel in the church of San Francesco in Pescia (by Andrea di Lazzaro Cavalcanti, known as il Buggiano, who was Brunelleschi's adopted son) or that of the Portuguese Cardinal's chapel at San Miniato al Monte (by Antonio Manetti Ciaccheri, once a disciple of Brunelleschi's).

While all this was going on more or less openly in Florence in the 1470s, the young Giuliano da Sangallo was in Rome studying the ancient ruins with Albertian eyes, reordering them into organic graphic works capable of influencing future architecture in the first instance theoretically, and later practically.

Lorenzo's particular construction vocabulary began to find its voice once he had come to power after the Pazzi Conspiracy in 1478, with his passion for walling. However, because of increasing financial constraints not only on his own family but, more importantly, on Florence in general, this was less all-consuming than in the case of his father Piero and particularly of his grandfather Cosimo. Having been influenced by Piero the Gouty and Alberti's generation, he was fond of precious materials such as polychrome marbles, modelled and painted stuccoes, relief sculpture for friezes and mirrors, and mosaics, and of the most complex antique architectural solutions where, for example, supporting columns were no longer arched in the medieval manner, but carried horizontal trabeations, superimposed and concatenated orders and archaeological references.

The not inconsiderable task of creating a concept capable of being transmitted directly from Florence to all the main Italian Humanist courts from Aragon Naples to Sforza Milan and Sixtus IV's Rome fell to Lorenzo. His too was the task of realizing Alberti's equally Humanistic dream of promoting architecture from its medieval position as a technical craft attractive as that was (yet again one is reminded of Brunelleschi), to a position of equal dignity to that held by painting, sculpture, literature and poetry – superior even, by dint of its philosophical ability to prove a theoretical (*per verba*) reason for its existence, not a characteristic of the other arts.

In fact, Giuliano da Sangallo who, with his courtly manners and his impeccable intellectual resources could hold his own with kings and princes (which he did, as Lorenzo's aesthetic ambassador to Naples and Milan, and later to the King of France), appears to be just as much a creature of Lorenzo's making as a product of his own fervent study of the principles of the *De Re Aedificatoria*.

Marsilio Ficino's neo-Platonism, the most popular philosophy of the time, did not surface during Lorenzo's rise to power by mere chance. In fact it seemed to be going in the same direction as the new construction ethic discussed above, if not actually anticipatory of it. It is a case of a style of architecture that existed in the creator-demiurge mind long before it was transformed into bricks and mortar, far from the compulsory building procedures of Brunelleschi's great workshops, a case of voluntary, deliberate dematerialization of the act of conception from the art of construction – which found, not by chance, an even more scandalous and clearer expression in Pico della Mirandola's *Commento sopra una Canzone De Amore*. Here the philosopher affirms that "the architect has within himself and in his mind the shape of the building he wishes to construct, and keeping that in mind as an example, produces and composes his own work. This shape is known by the Platonists as the Idea and the Example, and they would like the shape of the building in the mind of the creator to be more perfect and real than the [built] creation realized in materials… such as marble or stone etc.".

The works commissioned by Lorenzo and his cultured entourage carry this ideological baggage with them, a prerequisite for any attempt to interpret their own significance and underlying meaning and vital for the man in the street desirous of recognizing his own intellectual aspirations in them. It comes as no surprise, therefore, that the new temples, the churches that rose up within the inspiring Laurentian climate, no longer adhered to the traditional basilica style with triple naves divided by columns carrying arches, so typical of the early Christian and medieval traditions which Brunelleschi himself never quite renounced. They owe more to the classically-based very modern typology that Alberti discussed in his Treatise. Thus Giuliano da Sangallo conceived great halls with a single nave and square side chapels, along the lines of the Badia Fiesolana (and also the Chiesa di Cestello, later the church of Santa Maria Maddalena dei Pazzi in the Borgo Pinti, with its flat ceiling, and the church of the Convento di Sangallo [now lost] which was probably covered with a wide barrel vault). He also favoured even more modern ancient-style central plans: now octagons (like the sacristy in Santo Spirito, begun in 1488, or the huge sanctuary in the church of the Madonna dell'Umiltà in Pistoia, begun in 1492) with Albertian atria with barrel vaults and lacunars, or in the shape of a Greek cross (as, symbolically, in the church of the Madonna delle Carceri in Prato, begun in 1485).

Similarly, the new palaces which were the exclusive residences of the Laurentian elite are invested with a completely different livery to that of the hulking great tetragons so typical of the age of Brunelleschi and Michelozzo (see the palaces built for Cosimo de' Medici and Luca Pitti, clad in an intractable layer of rusticated ashlar). Their shaggy shapes are reminiscent of the medieval noblemen's homes of the mid-15th century and whose rather belated swan song was the colossal palace built for Filippo Strozzi. As early as the beginning of the 1450s, Alberti's facade for Giovanni Rucellai's palace with its classical articulation of the three superimposed orders of Doric, Ionic and Corinthian pilasters, was an expression of the resurgence of ancient ideas regenerated through a more philologically aware Humanistic approach. This proposed a much more modern alternative to the traditional facings of rusticated ashlar (see above) – an alternative that was given scant consideration in Florence, although it enjoyed as much success as the aesthetic beauty attributed to its linguistic counterpart in the other Renaissance centres such as Pius II's Pienza, Federico di Montefeltro's Urbino, Gonzaga's Mantua and Sixtus IV's Rome. Lorenzo it was, therefore, who attempted to redress this imbalance and tried to reconcile Florence with the ancient orders, taking advantage of his privileged position by trying out his ideas on the residences of those who were variously attached to his court, united by their cultural and aesthetic leanings. Thus it was that, within the suburban residence built by Giuliano da Sangallo for Bartolomeo Scala in Borgo Pinti near the old Arnolfo walls, the magnificent courtyard adorned with a concatenation of pilasters (used in place of the archaic arched supporting columns) and Bertoldo's great 'Platonic' stucco reliefs, became a focal point for meetings to which Marsilio Ficino was won to come.

Sangallo's own house, also on Borgo Pinti, was a true artist's home and it was there that the new building techniques were experimented with, such as that of using barrel vaults with lacunars over rectangular spaces (as described in some detail, although not in this context, in Alberti's *Treatise*), rather than the traditional system of chambered canopies with lunettes. The Agostinis followed a design apparently by Sangallo for their new palace (later Palazzo Cocchi) in front of the Basilica of Santa Croce, on the Piazza of the same name, which is simply an extremely faithful transposition in stone of the Albertian houses depicted in the anonymous *Tavole* in Urbino, Baltimore and Berlin. Their artist was certainly Florentine and closely linked to Giuliano da Sangallo or Botticelli, and as far as the depiction of the architecture is concerned, the 'painter's hand' would appear to be that of Sangallo himself.

Lorenzo could therefore be regarded as the patron Alberti never had and who deliberately tried to repay the debt that Florence, with its "great discarding" of Alberti's antique expertise, had contracted with its building history. It was Lorenzo who financed the publishing of the first edition of Alberti's *De Re Aedificatoria* in 1485, which was clearly bedtime reading for him, given his very highly developed sense of architectural patronage.

The privileged relationship between Lorenzo and Alberti was of vital importance, and it is biographically confirmed by accounts of the famous cavalcade of 1471 when the young Lorenzo, who had been in a position of power in Florence for barely two years, found himself in Rome as representative of the Republic during the crucial election of Sixtus IV. With the other young offspring of the city's oligarchy he took part in a prophetic architectural reconnaissance on horseback. Bernardo Rucellai describes the episode in his *De Urbe Roma* at the latter end of the century, during which the now very elderly artist summarized his long years of architectural and antiquarian experience in one unforgettable lesson.

Theirs was a relationship based on mutual admiration which presumably influenced Lorenzo's decision to try and acquire the property of his very close friends the Rucellai family at Poggio a Caiano several years later. Bernardo, the young son of the great Giovanni Rucellai was the same age as Lorenzo and husband of his sister, Nannina de' Medici. The bill of sale for the estate was accompanied by a drawing (a preliminary sketch for a project) which amplified an idea of somebody who was now dead. It would appear that the name, which is not given, was well known to both parties. This hypothetical development was to have been gardens above the loggia, the last plan to have been conceived by Alberti for the Rucellai family, which had the key function of providing the

original villa of Poggio a Caiano with hanging gardens reminiscent of those of antiquity (of which the most famous are the Gardens of Semiramide in Babylon, one of the Seven Wonders of the World). Apart from this strong sign of the modern desire to resurrect the notion of the ancient hanging gardens, Lorenzo's villa at Poggio a Caiano was a fundamental example of his great stylistic influence on the architecture of the late 15th century (in terms of Alberti's classicism) with particular reference to antique architecture. This influence was not confined to Florence: the Ionic pedimented portico of the main entrance, centred on the raised podium gives an impression of an octastyle temple – this was the first time the templar scheme, complete with triangular pediment, had been adapted for use on secular buildings, having previously been confined to buildings in religious use. The Ionic orders too, would have been seen by Horace's *mediocritas* as befitting men dedicated to the arts and study.

The large *salone* in the middle of the villa, covered by the largest barrel vaulted ceiling in Humanistic architectural history, would appear to be the realization of the Vitruvian concept of the "oeco corinzio", the monumental banqueting hall of the Roman *domus* or what Alberti described in his Treatise as the nerve centre, the vaulted heart of the villa which replaced the more traditional porticoed open courtyards.

Finally Lorenzo, still accompanied by his faithful Giuliano, also left his mark on the ordering of urban spaces, although it has to be said that Giuliano's original scheme never actually reached fruition, both because of the difficulties inherent in such enterprises for individual clients – even though this particular one was so powerful – and because of the undeniably unhealthy state of Florence's economy at the end of the century. Lorenzo was basically concerned with organizing the entire north east area of the city (between the present Via Gino Capponi, Via della Colonna, Borgo Pinti and the Viali which now provide a ring road on the area where the Arnolfo walls once stood). He erected exemplary buildings (modern convents such as that at Cestello and private quality houses, such as those of Sangallo and Bartolomeo Scala), laying out the streets according to a rational orthogonal plan (viz the crossroads between streets such as the symptomatic Via Laura and Via della Pergola, between Borgo Pinti and Via degli Alfani and so on), and planning low-cost buildings on sites prudently acquired by the Medici family which would then be sold or let.

In the centre of this 'new' Florence, Giuliano da Sangallo had been due to erect the new family palace, no longer ponderously weighted down by the medieval volumetry of Michelozzo and Brunelleschi's cubic castellations, but based on an expanded vision of the homes of the Ancients, with the main body of the building articulated round a courtyard destined for theatrical or chivalresque entertainments (with steps going up all four sides, as in theatres), and rectangular, square and round rooms (a virtual reproposition of the complex Imperial villas and thermae) which would then be completely surrounded by gardens, or "xisti" as Vitruvius would have them. This plan was probably submitted to Lorenzo's son Giovanni, once, as Pope Leo X, he had won back the state of Florence in 1513.

As can well be seen, Lorenzo's architectural intentions were highly ambitious, aimed at a rapid and thorough modernization of the vocabulary and function of architecture.

Lorenzo's aspirations were thwarted by financial difficulties and then by his early death and the consequent political overthrowing of the Medici family, although they planted very fertile seeds in the mind of his son Giovanni, who was created Cardinal at a very tender age. As Pope Leo X, he managed to execute faithfully all his father's plans in Rome, with the aid of Bramante, Raphael and Michelangelo, from the modern system of orders to the antique decoration not just of the outside but also of the inside of the sumptuous 'courts' so as to render them even more magnificent. There was the antique villa of Villa Madama (with its volumetric structure and its partly hanging gardens), a paradigm of extraordinary good fortune both for Italy and for Europe, the myth of the central plan, the desire to bestow a hegemonizing role on the architectural Treatises (of both Alberti and Vitruvius), until the logic of classicist rationalization extended not just to single buildings but to whole areas of the city.

It no longer seems paradoxical to state that the Rome of the *Renovatio Imperii* and the *Instauratio Urbis* during the glorious twenty to twenty-five years of the Cinquecento (Medici for the most part) has its roots firmly embedded it the aesthetic concepts and intellectual aspirations of Laurentian Florence at the end of the Quattrocento.

Selected Bibliography

K. von Stegmann, H. von Geymüller: *Die Architektur der Renaissance in Toskana*, 11 vol., Munich 1885-1909.

W. Limburger: *Die Gabaude von Florenz*, Leipzig 1910.

A. Venturi: *Storia dell'arte italiana*, VI, *L'Architettura del Quattrocento*, Milan 1926.

R. Wittkower: *Architectural Principles in the Age of Humanism*, London 1949.

A. Chastel: *Art et Humanisme à Florence au temps de Laurent le Magnifique*, Paris 1959.

P. Sanpaolis: 'La casa fiorentina di Bartolomeo Scala', in *Studien zur toskanischen Kunst. Festschrift für L.H. Reidenreich*, Munich 1964.

M. Martelli: 'I pensieri architettonici di Lorenzo il Magnifico', in *Commentari*, XVII, 1966.

G. Miarelli Mariani: 'Il disegno per il complesso mediceo di Via Laura a Firenze', in *Palladio*, s.n., 1-4 (1972).

P.H. Foster: *A Study of Lorenzo de' Medici's Villa at Poggio a Caiano*, Ph. D. Dissertation, Yale University, 1974.

F. Borsi: *Leon Battista Alberti: L'opera completa*, Milan 1975.

C. Elam: 'Lorenzo de' Medici and Urban development of Renaissance Florence', *Art History*, I, 1 (1978).

F.W. Kent: 'New light on Lorenzo de' Medici's Convent at Porta San Gallo', *The Burlington Magazine*, CXXIV (1982).

M. Ferrara, F. Quinterio: *Michelozzo di Bartolomeo*, Florence 1984.

S. Borsi: *Giuliano da Sangallo. I disegni di architettura e dell'antico*, Rome 1985.

S. Borsi, F. Quinterio, C. Vasic Vatovec: *Maestri fiorentini nei cantieri romani del Quattrocento*, S. Danesi Squarzina (ed.), Rome 1989.

H. Günter: *Das Studium der Antiken Architektur in den Zeichnungen der Hoch Renaissance*; Tübingen 1988.

G. Morolli: 'Lorenzo, Leonardo e Giuliano: da San Lorenzo al Duomo a Poggio a Caiano', *QUASAR*, 3, 1990.

'Per bellezza, per studio, per piacere'. Lorenzo il Magnifico e gli spazi dell'arte, F. Borsi (ed.), Florence 1991.

G. Morolli, C. Acidini Luchinat, L. Marchetti (ed.), *L'architettura di Lorenzo il Magnifico*, Exhibition catalogue (Florence), Milan 1992.

Lorenzo, Alberti and the Florentine Architectonic Treatises
Gabriele Morolli

One might quite reasonably have expected as radical an aesthetic "revolution" as that of Brunelleschi and his followers to have been consolidated by some sort of written text – this, however, appears not to have been the case, indeed the architectonic theory of Florence during the first period of Humanism is singularly weak. Brunelleschi published no treatises, neither did Michelozzo.

Ghiberti alone, who was not as great an exponent of the revolutionary Humanist principles, and whose artistry tended to uphold the glorious traditions of 14th century art even during the period of renewal of the Renaissance, puts forward a few general ideological proposals in the section devoted to the art of building in his *Commentarii*, which in turn owe much to the theories expounded by Vitruvius in his *De Architectura*. Significantly, one could say that all the Florentine treatises are the result of a state of exile: one has only to think of Filarete, who wrote *Sforzinda* while he was actually in Milan, still under Sforza rule in the 1450 and 1460s. Then there is Alberti who had grown up in exile in Padua, part of the very cultured pre-humanist Republic of Venice, who returned to Florence during the 1430s, once the family ban was lifted, and sprung fully armed, rather as Minerva sprung from Jove's head, onto Florence's aesthetic stage.

The only constant genre of artistic literature throughout the century was the production of biographies, lives of the artists, which were crammed with information and details of craftsmanship. These connected Cennino Cennini's pre-humanist *Libro dell'Arte* and Filippo Villani's *De Origine Civitatis Florentiae et giusdem famosis civibus* (circa 1400) with the proto-historiographical information contained in Ghiberti's *Commentarii* (circa 1450) and the *Laudatio* of Florentine civilization that heralded Cristoforo Landino's great edition of Dante's *Commedia* (1481). This tradition culminated in the precious writings of Vasari's so-called precursors, Anonimo Magliabechiano, and the proto-Cinquecentesque Antonio Billi and Anonimo Gaddiano.

It was Alberti who instituted the genre of architectonic literature which was to remain characteristic of Italian and European Classicism until at least the19th century. Very little of the sort had been published before Alberti's systematic and 'very modern' series of treatises, which were published between 1435 and 1452. This comprised *De Pictura/Della Pictura*, *De Statua* and *De Re Aedificatoria*, as well as the *Descriptio Urbis Romae*, which was a periegetic archaeological survey which included graphic and topographical references.

Alberti's *De Re Aedificatoria* was really an attempt to 'modernize' Vitruvius' theories, transforming the Latin. The illustrious patrons who claimed to have copies were Bernardo Bembo, Federico da Montefeltro, Matthius Corvinus, the Medici family, the Aragons of Naples and the Estensi family of Ferrara.

It would seem, therefore, that from the very first, the princes had singled out Alberti's Treatise as being one of the most efficient socio-political instruments for the modern interpretation of their prestigious homes as lordly cornerstones of the Renaissance centres of Urbino, Rome, Ferrara and Mantua, although their application proved somewhat problematic in Florence. They were benchmarks of the deliberate strategy of cultural politics, where the new ancient building style served as a prime metaphorical indicator of the effectiveness of the patrons' seigneurial power and social standing. Even theoretically speaking, the, divorce between Brunelleschi's city and Alberti's culture is perfectly obvious, at least as regards the general resilience of the Florentines (with the sole exception of the Rucellai family) to Alberti's own architectural proposals.

It still remains, however that the extremely modern Alberti, in spite of encountering great hostility in the early stages of his career, took the winning side (or to be more precise, the side that was to emerge victorious many years later) of the new culture that was not merely aesthetic but also ideological and philosophical. This was the side of Neoplatonism, which was so important to the evolution of architectonic shapes in the mid-15th century. It comes as no surprise, therefore, that in Cristoforo Landini's *Disputationes Camaldulenses* of 1460, which purport to be reports of Neoplatonist discussions held at Camaldoli, Alberti is reported as upholding the superiority of the contemplative life as against the active life in a debate with the young Lorenzo de' Medici who is, equally significantly, arguing the other side.

In a similar exercise to the archaeological cavalcade of 1471, "duce Baptista Alberti", is reported by Bernardo Rucellai as having launched Lorenzo on the road to the appreciation of ancient architecture. His maieutic Neoplatonist itinerary would have been designed to cause him to develop an attitude more conscious of "ratiocinatio" (the consideration of theory in tandem with Vitruvius' definition of "arte edificatoria" and the above-mentioned "fabrica"), once he had shaken off the facile myths of the architectural hegemony of the Vitruvian "fabric" on theoretical reflection, of the quality of workmanship being the single most important factor in the art of building, and of Brunelleschi's ideal of the supremacy of the artist as craftsman. Alberti advocated the importance of the relationship of a project to its surroundings, even at the conceptual stage, of the idea of a style of architecture that might vanquish the tetragonal style of building, weighed down by its material construction of stone and lime. Even in architecture, therefore, the "Litterae Operosae" of the early Quattrocento were discarded in favour of the hyper-Uranian "calm" and "tranquillity" in which those caught up in the discussions on the "sommo bene" consciously sought refuge.

The basic underlying principles of the *De Re Aedificatoria* need to be taken and examined separately from its effectual and significant analogies with Vitruvius' *De Architectura*. There is a Neoplatonist sub plot: there are the two souls of the art of building itself, the "intelligible" soul of the ideological world, institutionalized by the ancient theoretical texts (Vitruvius), the other "sensitive" soul of the immense, basically classical canonical vocabulary of the ancient buildings.

There was a marked dualism in the binomial question of the relationship between proportion and order. The former guarantees the mathematical and geometrical harmony of the architectural forms, and the more generally numerical "concert" of the entire universe according to Pythagoras. The latter is the demonstration of these harmonies through a codified, recognizable, repeatable and secure morphology.

Alberti's startling reference to building as a great living organism or "animal", architectonically representative of the myth of the "soul of the world" appears to have been a much more serious hermeneutic approach than the extrinsic, though fascinating, anthropomorphism of Francesco di Giorgio. Di Giorgio's penchant was for incorporating seductive human shapes into the geometrical plans of cities, fortresses, basilicas and even into the profiles or outlines of columns, and members of various sorts.

It is hardly surprising, therefore, that in spite of a rather lukewarm reception, *De Re Aedificatoria* was the only 15th century architectural treatise to published. Lorenzo de'Medici, Alberti's patron, not only financed publication in 1485, but also volunteered the editorial services of his man of letters and poet Angelo Poliziano. Alberti was not discovered by Lorenzo, but the publication of his Treatise was the jewel in the crown of an aesthetic relationship that had lasted for nearly twenty years between the great Alberti on the one hand and the *Signore* of Florence with his intellectual elite headed by Giuliano da Sangallo, on the other.

Lorenzo's affection for Alberti is referred to in the correspondence between his secretaries and Ercole I d'Este in 1484, on the subject of *De Re Aedificatoria*. They mention that the Prince "is very fond of him and it is read by him", saying that when Lorenzo was taking the waters at the Bagni di San Filippo, sheets of printed paper would arrive, which were the proofs of the book then being printed in Florence. "Every day I read to Lorenzo but soon we will run out", they continue, adding that it would therefore be necessary to send more "by the first horseman" to leave Florence bound for the spa's revivifying attractions.

Although Laurentian Florence was a city abounding in creativity (there was a smaller volume of buildings than at the beginning of the century, but they were of much higher quality), it was also extremely rich in terms of architectonic literature.

Apart from Alberti's extraordinary impact and Vitruvius' surviving Treatise, the age of Lorenzo saw the birth of a new kind of architectonic theorizing with the publication of treatises in the form of sketchbooks. These were to become very popular in the 16th century, with the collections of drawings of ancient Rome by Serlio, Labacco, Pirro Ligorio, Palladio, Jacques-Androuet Du Cerceau and so on. Alberti had started off this new tradition with his *Descriptio Urbis Romae*, and Giuliano da Sangallo then followed suit with his *Libro* and his *Taccuino*. These were regarded not just as collections of purely personal and private sketches that the artists had made for future use, jealously guarded as secret models and unsuspected sources of inspiration. Above all they were a deliberate *suite* of ancient materials, detailed enough to be re-used in designs that were not merely of accidental and ephemeral value, but were being saved up for some specific and special project of the artist. They were permanent, definitive *exempla* on which the artists would reflect at length and they were a legacy for later disciples, just as instructive as the sentences and pages of a written architectonic treatise (to be studied in a Neoplatonistic atmosphere of "calm" and "tranquillity"). The only difference was that they used pictures rather than words.

The vogue for "taccuini" or sketchbooks was at its height between the end of the 15th century and the beginning of the 16th century. They were published by Ghirlandaio and del Cronaca, there were the Codices of Coner and Escurialense, and countless notebooks belonging to Raphael's disciples, some of which were anonymous, and so on. The precise maieutic aesthetic relevance of these sketchbooks can be tied into the equally architecturally didactic phenomen of the decorated study. This was the province not so much of the young painters, but of the cultured patrons, who liked to have their studies decorated with richly ornamented painted panels, most of which portrayed scenes from antiquity in which buildings were depicted with an extraordinarily detailed compositional knowledge.

Finally, yet another testament to the love of theory during the age of Lorenzo il Magnifico was the cultured Florentines' passion for studying Vitruvius' treatise, which counterbalanced the predominant historiographical prejudice in favour of the notion that the exegesis of *De Architectura* took place mainly in Rome and Venice. As early as the 14th century, Boccaccio and Petrarch were in possession of manuscript copies of the Latin treatise, as Cennino Cennini and Filippo Villani well knew. At the turn of the century the 'Vitruvius affair' came to the forefront of Florentine aesthetic debate once more, both because of the false discovery of Vitruvius' manuscript in the Biblioteca di Sangallo by Poggio Bracciolini in 1414, because of the legend of Francesco Alighieri and Bernardino Donati's versions, and because of the systematic plagiarizing of it by both Lorenzo Ghiberti, in his *Commentarii* and his nephew Buonaccorso in his *Zibaldone*. There were at least four other copies of *De Architectura* in the Medici collections in Florence and another copy, annotated by Poliziano, is known to have been in the Library of the Convento di San Marco. 14th century copies by Donato Acciaioli and Boccaccio (now lost) were known to have been circulating in Florence, as was a copy by Pico della Mirandola (also lost), not to mention the many copies made in Florence for the libraries of Bologna, Rome, Naples and other Humanist cities.

The Roman *editio princeps* of 1486 appears to revolve significantly around Albertian or Laurentian personalities, and the editors, Pomponio Leto and Sulpicio da Veroli appear to have had links with the cultural scene in Rome, where Alberti was becoming increasingly highly thought of. Cardinal Raffaele Riario was the cultured patron of this edition (he built the Palazzo Riario and the Cancelleria which appears to be an astute *conjunctio* between a Vitruvian *domus* and an Albertian-Urbinate palace/city) and had formed a coterie of intellectuals around his studio in Pisa (in the university revived by Lorenzo) where he met various members of Lorenzo's educated clique.

Florence, in turn, came to the inevitable point of publishing an edition of *De Architectura*, in which, as in Alberti's *De Re Aedificatoria*, the aspirations of the Laurentian generation were reflected, as in a theoretical/institutional diptych. Oddly enough, while scrupulously recording the first printed editions of the Latin treatise, historians have always tended to pay scant attention to the fact that the second edition not only spanned two years, 1495-1496, but that it was published in both Florence and Venice, with a third edition being published in Venice in 1497, just one year later. This was a prodrome of Fra Giocondo's new large illustrated 1511 edition of *De Architectura*, and subtly yet deliberately led to the *de facto* historiographical concept of the editorial hegemony of the Venetian Republic. Even Giocondo's edition was published in

Venice, rather than within the cultural ambience of Lorenzo's Florence, to which, in our opinion, the project should have been entrusted, from first concept to final edition.

A study of other works published at the same time as this innovative edition of *De Architectura* must inevitably include Julius Frontinus' *De Aquaeductibus* and two works (*Panepistemon* and *Lamia*) by Poliziano, editor of the 1485 *De Re Aedificatoria*, who died in 1494. Five woodcut designs were included in the Giocondo's edition for the very first time (both the Sulpicio *editio princeps* and the manuscript tradition of treatises were texts completely devoid of illustration). In 1495 Francesco Cattani da Diacceto, who took over the running of Ficino's Platonic Academy at Careggi, succeeded in being granted an editorial privilege for the publication of a "Vitruvio in Architettura, cum el greco et figure sue non piu stampato". Giocondo's version, with all the editorial work it entailed, would therefore appear to be of great historiographical relevance. This all took place, in fact, at a time when the Medici regime in Florence was being taken over by a 'Neomedievalist' Republic inspired by Savonarola, and this edition which formed the basis for Classicism, a 'Bible' destined to spread the word about ancient building methods, assumes an extraordinary importance. It is even possible that the citation of Venice as a place of printing (in addition to Florence) could well be nothing else than a piece of *escamotage* destined to attract censure by the anticlassical and anti-Medici Republican factions (given the number of suspect editions printed during the 16th century in hundreds and hundreds of European cities). It would appear, however, from the toponym on the frontispiece to have actually been published in one of the many sympathetic cities in free Switzerland.

This, even at the level of cultural politics constituted a crude betrayal of the principles of classical Laurentian culture, which was declared to be one of "paganism" *tout court*. The remaining members of Ficino's coterie of Neoplatonist and pro-Medici followers from the Platonic Academy at Careggi were mobilized into creating a treatise that was to be a *pièce de résistance* against the pre-Lutheran piety of the Piagnoni. They had their headquarters in the gardens of the Orti Oricellari, and were led by Bernardo Rucellai, who was the son of Giovanni Rucellai, one of Alberti's great patrons as well as being the same age as Lorenzo de'Medici and one of his closest friends (he had even married Lorenzo's sister Nannina).

It was a case, therefore, of one might call an Oricellarian Vitruvius, the late – if not very late – fruit of the Laurentian passion for the antique, gathered together within the Rucellai garden walls. One way or another, the Rucellai had kept Florence's contact with classical and ancient culture alive for a good fifty years. This was a powerful antidote to the continual risk of this wonderful city becoming self-satisfied and provincial, and content with its own immeasurable glories. But, during the second half of the 16th century, this parabola was to start describing Florence's melancholy yet mesmerizing decline.

The Medici family were fond of the works of Vitruvius, which seemed to reflect their own particular culture and ideology, and this is confirmed by the fact that in 1513, the year Leo X took back the Signoria of the city, the Giunta press published a new edition of the very recent Venetian version of Giocondo's 1511 *De Architectura*. It was not simply a matter of publishing another edition, but it was a whole new undertaking in that the format was changed from quarto to octave, which in turn led to the engravings having to be remade. The likelihood that this new 'pocket edition' would have a much wider circulation also had to be taken into account. The fact that Frontinius' *De Aquaeductibus* had been included in the Oricellarian edition of 1495-1496, and that it was part of the new Florentine version of *De Architectura*, whereas Giocondo had neglected to include it in his 1511 Vitruvius, is not insignificant.

In approximately 1520, advised by a rather cantankerous Michelangelo, Pier Vettori started collecting the avant-garde of the best Tuscan theoretical essays for himself and his famous library. Gherardo Spini records in 1568 that knowledgeable artists and connoisseurs of architecture "saw and examined many of Vitruvius' writings and it came about that for diverse reasons this study

remained incomplete". Pier Vettori, in fact, owned the precious translation of *De Architectura* that Raphael had commissioned from Fabio Calvi with the intention of publishing it along with his own annotations. All this extraordinary exegetic material is now in Monaco.

Then there was the dramatic siege of 1527, when the Medici resorted to the power of weapons as *instrumentum regni* rather than culture. Michelangelo finally left for Rome in 1533, and, along with many other aspiring intellectuals, the groups of Vitruvius' followers were silenced, although their echo continued to reverberate well into the late 1530s, when the works of Giovanni Norchiati were lost. Norchiati had been a great friend of Michelangelo's and a Canon of the Medici church of San Lorenzo, where the extraordinary Library, built on designs by Michelangelo for Leo X and Clement VII, was striving to reach completion before the shock of the Sack.

By then the cult of the treatise had moved from Florence to Rome where the disciples of the Accademia della Virtù, as well as Giuliano da Sangallo's nephews Antonio the Younger and his brother Giovan Battista were attempting dreary and doomed efforts at translating, illustrating and evaluating *De Architectura*, before Venice stole the limelight once more, producing by far the most successful edition – that by Daniele Barbaro with woodcuts by Palladio.

There can be no doubt that the fervent Classical theorizing which took place in Rome and Venice also had its brilliance, even if this was occasionally overshadowed, in Lorenzo's Florence.

Selected Bibliography

G.K. Lukomsky: *I maestri dell'architettura classica da Vitruvio allo Scamozzi*, Milan 1933.

R. Wittkower: *Architectural Principles in the Age of Humanism*, London 1949.

A. Chastel: *Arte e Umanesimo a Firenze al tempo di Lorenzo il Magnifico*, Turin 1959.

L.B. Alberti: *L'Architettura*, G. Orlandi, P. Portoghesi (ed.), Milan 1966.

C.H. Krinky: 'Seventy-eight Vitruvius Manuscripts', *Journal of the Warburg and Courtauld Institutes*, XXX (1967), pp. 36-70.

Vitruvius on Architecture, F. Granger (ed.), Cambridge (Mass.), London 1970.

A. Averlino, named the Filarete: *Trattato di Architettura*, A.M. Finoli, L. Grassi (ed.), Milan 1972.

V. Juren: 'Politien et Vitruve', *Rinascimento*, XVIII (1978), pp. 285-293.

L. Vagnetti, L. Marcucci: 'Per una co-

scienza vitruviana e Regesto cronologico e critico delle edizioni', in 2000 'Anni di Vitruvio', s.n., *Studi e Documenti di Architettura*, VIII (1978), pp. 11-193.

Vitruvii De Architectura Libri Decem, C. Fensterbusch (ed.), Darmstadt 1981.

G. Morolli: *"Le Membra degli Ornamenti". Dizionario illustrato degil ordini architettonici*, Florence 1986.

V. Fontana: *Fra Giovanni Giocondo architetto, 1433 c. - 1515*, Vicenza 1988.

G. Morolli: *L'Architettura di Vitruvio. Una guida illustrata*, 2 vol. Florence 1988

AA.VV.: *Les Traités d'Architecture de la Renaissance*, Tours, 1st-11th July 1981, Paris 1988.

'Per bellezza, per studio, per piacere'. Lorenzo il Magnifico e gli spazi dell'arte, F. Borsi (ed.), Florence 1991.

G. Morolli, C. Acidini Luchinat, L. Marchetti (ed.), *L'architettura di Lorenzo il Magnifico*, Exhibition catalogue (Florence), Milan 1992.

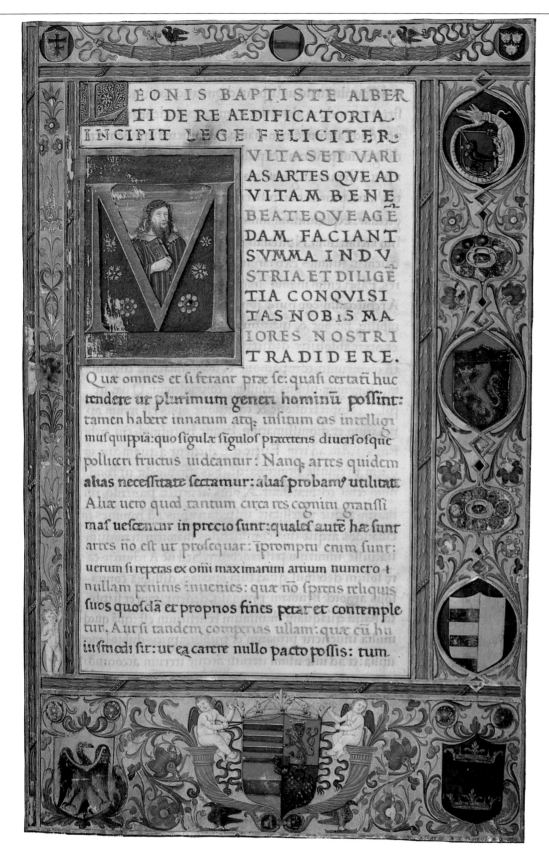

Leon Battista Alberti
De Re Aedificatoria,
second half 15th century
Modena, Biblioteca Estense cod.
alpha 0.3.8

LEONIS BAPTISTE ALBERTI DE RE AEDIFICA
TORIA INCIPIT LEGE FELICITER

VLTAS ET VARIAS ARTES QVE
ad uitam bene beatéq; agédam faciant summa
industria et diligentia conquisitas nobis ma
iores nostri tradidere. Quae omnes et si ferant
prae se:quasi certatim huc tendere:Vt pluri
mum generi hominum prosint:tamen habere
innatum atq; insitum eas intelligimus quip
piam:quo singulae singulos praeceteris diuersosq; polliceri fruc
tus uideantur:Nanq; artes quidem alias necessirate sectamur:
alias probamus utilitate:Aliae uero qp tantum circa res cogniti
gratissimas uersentur in pretio sunt:quales autem hae sint artes
non est ut prosequar:inpromptu enim sunt:uerum si repetas ex
omni maximarum artium numero nullam penitus inuenies:quae
non spretis reliquis suos quosdam & proprios fines petat et con
templetur. Aut si tandem comperias ullam:quae cum huiusmodi
sit:ut ea carere nullo pacto possis:tum et de se utilitatem:uolup
tati dignitatiq; ɔiunctam praestet:meo iudicio ab earum numero
excludendam esse:non duces architecturam:namq; ea quidem
siquidem rem diligentius pensitaris et publice & priuatim com
modissima et uehementer gratissima generi hominum est:digni
tateq; inter primas non postrema:Sed anteq; ultra progrediar:
explicandum mihi censeo quemnam haberi uelim architectum:
Non enim tignarium adducam fabrū:quem tu summis caeteraq;
disciplinarum uiris compares:Fabri enim manus architecto pro
instrumento e.Architectum ego hunc fore constituam:qui certa
admirabiliq; ratione et uia tum mente animoq; diffinire:tum et
opere absoluere didicerit quecunq; ex ponderum motu corpoq;q;
compactione et coagmentatione dignissimis hominū usibus bel
lissime cōmodentur:Quae ut possit cōprehensione et cognitione
opus est rerum optimarum et dignissimaq;:Itaq; huiusmodi erit
architectus:redeo ad rem Fuere qui dicerent aquam aut ignem

a i

**Leonis Baptistae Alberti Florentini
viri clorissimi de Re Aedificatoria
opus elegantisssimum et quam
maxime utile**, NICCOLÒ DI LORENZO
ALAMANNO, FIRENZE.
First printed folio edition of the
treatise, with dedication by Angelo
Poliziano to Lorenzo il Magnifico

M. Vitruvius Pollio
De Architectura
15th century
Small quarto volume in paper,
Medicean binding in red morocco,
comprising 137 leaves and two outer
endpapers (180 x 260 mm),
containing the complete text, except
the Greek verses, of Vitruvius' De
Architectura
Florence, Biblioteca Medicea
Laurenziana (Plut. 30.12)

VITRUVIUS POLLIO: Marcus: De
architecture. [Followed by:] **Angelo
POLIZIANO, Panepistemon; Lamia;
FRONTINUS, De aquaeductibus**
Florence, [Venice, Cristoforo de'
Pensi], 1495, 1496, 310 x 210 mm,
85 leaves
Handwritten note on reverse of leaf
no. 1. The work is bound with:
CELSUS, Aurelius Cornelius, De
Medicina. Venice, F. Pinzi,
published by B. Fontana, 1497, XCI
leaves [3]
Biblioteca Nazionale Centrale
di Firenze, Inc.C.2.11ᵃ
(Work without illustration)

**L'Architettura di Leonbattista
Alberti tradotta in lingua fiorentina
da Cosimo Bartoli […]** CON
L'AGGIUNTA DE' DISEGNI, **Lorenzo
Torrentino, Firenze**
1550
(The architecture of Leon Battista
Alberti translated into the Florentine
by Cosimo Bartoli […] including
designs, Lorenzo Torrentino,
Florence)
First illustrated Italian edition, in
folio, edited by Cosimo Bartoli
("supported" by Francesco
Campana) and offered to Cosimo I
de' Medici, the Duke of Florence. 82
woodcuts, attributed to Vasari's close
circle (the beautiful frontispiece is
certainly the work of Giorgio Vasari)

**Wooden Model with the
Restoration of the Original
Appearance of the Villa at Poggio
a Caiano**
F. Gizdulich, 1992
scale 1:50, 106 x 107 x 30 cm

The Public Life

The Church and the City in 15th Century Florence
Paolo Viti

The year 393 AD was of momentous importance in the religious and civil history of Florence. This was the year in which the suburban church of San Lorenzo was consecrated first cathedral of the city in the presence of Ambrogio, Bishop of Milan. This was proof of the fact that Florence, built by the Roman republicans on the banks of the Arno, had now acquired a physiognomy of its own and a specific role within the surrounding territory. Prior to this, the older city of Fiesole had always had more cachet. By the end of the 4th century and the beginning of the 5th century Florence might have been in a position to elect a bishop of great pastoral piety, Zanobi, who would have been the most famous bishop of Roman times and, later, patron of the diocese.

The subsequent unfolding of the history of Florence does not appear to differ greatly from the general pattern of events throughout Tuscany and Italy. Charlemagne, who was elevated to the rank of Emperor by Leo III on Christmas night 800, appears to have organized the restoration of the walls of Florence previously destroyed by the Lombards. Although the city chose St John the Baptist as its Patron Saint during the course of the 11th century it was not until 1250, with the death of the Emperor Frederick II, who had conducted a campaign of devastation in Florence in 1238, that Florence began to develop its constitutional form.

As early as the beginning of the middle of the 9th century the religious life of the Florentine people was distinguished by new developments that revealed their great inner strength and their capacity for communal life. The convents of the great monastic orders, such as Badia a Settignano and Certosa del Galluzzo are an example of this, as are the mendicant Orders. During the 12th century Franciscans, Dominicans, Carmelites, Heremites, Humiliati, Servites and the Camaldolese all erected their own monasteries within the city environs, these often became focuses for the cultural and spiritual life of the whole city.

It is not hard to understand how at the end of the 13th century and the beginning of the 14th century, such an all-pervading religious ambience inspired Dante Alighieri and Giotto, both Florentines, to attempt, albeit in different ways, to steer their peers towards the paths of spiritual and moral righteousness. This righteousness was pursued even more vigorously in 15th century Florence by Petrarch's humanist followers' displays of absolute originality and extra-ordinary force. It is not mere chance that in Florence, particularly during the first ten years of the Quattrocento, there were very long debates on the advisability or otherwise of reading pagan literature rather than the Scriptures. Highly spiritual men such as Cardinal Giovanni Dominici (who founded the convent at San Domenico in 1408) took part in these debates against the humanists who, led by Coluccio Salutati, had grown tired of the scholastic tradition and the now inadequate medieval interpretations. At the same time, there was a new school of thought, originated by the Camaldolese Friar Ambrogio Traversari (Vicar General of the Order): the re-establishment of the patristic texts as the perfect humanist guides to the Greek language. These were some of the major milestones in the secular life of the Florentine Church before 1419 when, under Bishop Amerigo Corsini, Pope Martin V established the city as an Archbishopric and a metropolitan see.

Florence's standing during this period was so high, due to its exceptional cultural status and economic superiority, achieved as a result of the activities of the Medici Bank who had been bankers to the Church for some time, that Pope Eugenius IV fled there from Rome in 1434. In 1439, the Council of Basle met there as a result of a financial incentive from Cosimo de'Medici, which led to a short-lived union between the Greek and Latin Churches. The new cathedral of Santa Maria del Fiore had been consecrated in 1436, giving a new lease of spiritual and political life to the city.

Civil life in Florence in its various forms continued to maintain close links with religious life. The Dominican Friar Leonardo Dati, Vicar General from 1414, was engaged several times by the city's governors on diplomatic missions. Whilst some of Florence's most illustrious families became patrons of churches, the Medici decorated the church of San Lorenzo and the convent of San Marco, the Strozzi and the Sassetti contributed towards the church of Santa Trìnita, later the Rucellai aided the churches of Santa Maria Novella and San Pancrazio and the Pucci supported the church of Santissima Annunziata.

Unfortunately this fervour could not be said to have been offset by any sort of pastoral leadership from the Diocese: for years Archbishops had come from outside the city and were scarcely interested in what went on there, as in the case of Giovanni Vitelleschi, Ludovico Trevisan, Bartolomeo Zabarella (between 1435 and 1445) followed by Pietro Riario and Rinaldo Orsini (between 1473 and 1503). There were few Florentine Bishops: Antonino Pierozzi, Orlando Bonarli and Giovanni Neroni, between 1446 and 1473. As far as the faith of the city was concerned, Pierozzi (1446-1458) clearly took his pastoral duties very seriously and published numerous works of doctrine. In social and civil life, he was an active defender of the poor and underprivileged and therefore an advocate of those ethical rules dedicated to the prevention of political oppression by the ruling classes.

Bishop Pierozzi's term of office saw the gradual consolidation of

Cosimo de'Medici's position as first citizen of the city (1434-1464), and this was naturally reflected in the religious sector: not so much as regards Cosimo's enthusiasm for building new churches and convents as in the ecclesiastical political rule exercised under the aegis of the Bishop in the Florentine territorial dioceses as well as throughout Tuscany itself. It was hardly surprising then, that an increasing number of Bishops belonged to families allied with the Medici, thus guaranteeing control in yet another sphere within the cities in their power. This was still the situation in 1469, when Lorenzo de' Medici took over the political mantle from his father Piero (1464-1469), son of Cosimo. Under Lorenzo (1469-1492), the constitutional changes brought into force thirty years earlier achieved maximum effect, particularly as the reins of power were becoming increasingly limited to the Medici family. Their power was at its peak under Lorenzo, notably after the sack of Volterra in 1472, after the Pazzi conspiracy of 1478 and the subsequent war with Pope Sixtus IV. Finally, after the conflict with Rome had ceased, Lorenzo was able to concentrate on the internal politics of his city, increasingly dispensing with the old magistracies and gradually assuming absolute power himself.

An example of this was in 1489 when he obtained Pope Innocent VIII's promise (made public only three years later) of a cardinalate for his thirteen-year-old son, Giovanni, who later became Pope Leo X (1513-1521). Lorenzo saw his son's cardinalate as one of the greatest successes of his political career, one which opened up new avenues for the family: another Medici, Giulio, was later to become Pope Clement VII from 1523 to 1534.

Lorenzo's more notable successes aside, there are other examples of his power of decision as regards the nomination of Florentine archbishops. One of these was his brother-in-law, Rinaldo Orsini (1474-1503) who asked Lorenzo himself if he could be put in charge of the diocese: the choice of Orsini constituted a victory over one of the anti-Medici factions and its Archbishop Francesco Salviati, whom Lorenzo had not managed to avoid in Pisa.

It is easy to understand how Laurentian politicians, no great respecters of judicial law, often found opposition in the religious sector among those who preached the necessity of moral rectitude, the abandonment of corruption and violence and the safety and instruction of the human person. Thus, for example, Lorenzo wasted no time in banishing the monk Bernardino da Feltre from Florence because he was thought too dangerous with his vehement preaching, denouncing the degeneration of Florentine politics. On the contrary, he favoured another monk Mariano da Genazzano, whose homilies were more politically acceptable and whose elegant rhetoric was more seductive. In this political climate, the episode of the Dominican friar Girolamo Savonarola, called to Florence from Ferrara in 1489 by Lorenzo himself, appears to have been totally disruptive and guaranteed to throw the contradictions within the Florentine Church into violent relief. Savonarola not only criticized the established misgovernment of Florence, but also that of Rome under the current Pope Alexander VI. It appeared that the cities of both Rome and Florence were incapable, like Lorenzo and the pontiff, of achieving any sort of civil or religious reform. The dramatic conclusion of the Savonarola debacle, in 1498 – when he was burnt at the stake along with his most faithful henchmen, and their ashes thrown into the Arno – is a benchmark of the state of Florence at the end of the 15th century. Between 1494 and 1498 many of Savonarola's innovative and reformist theories were put to the test, even at a political level, and Savonarola's death was seen by many politicians as avenging the moral blackmail occasioned by the betrayal of Lorenzo's son Piero in 1494. These – and many other – milestones in the history of the Florentine Church caused an unprecedented coming together of cultural milieux and were greatly acclaimed, not just as religious subjects, by artists, painters, architects, sculptors, illustrators, and by masters of all the lesser-known art forms, as well as by men of letters, who knew how to interpret and give shape to the city's anxiety through their unique and peerless masterpieces, as can be seen from the small selection on show here.

Selected Bibliography

W. and E. Paatz: *Die Kirchen von Florenz*, Frankfurt am Main 1952.

N. Rubinstein: *Il governo di Firenze sotto i Medici (1434-1494)*, it. tr., Florence, 1971.

R.C. Trexler: *Synodal Law in Florence and Fiesole (1305-1518)*, Rome 1971.

D. Kent: *The Rise of the Medici. Faction in Florence (1426-1434)*, Oxford 1978.

L. Martines: *Lawyers and Statecraf in Renaissance Florence*, Princeton 1978.

R. Bizzocchi: *Chiesa e potere nella Toscana del Quattrocento*, Bologna 1987.

M.A. Morelli Timpanaro - R. Manno Tolu - P. Viti (ed.): *Consorterie politiche e mutamenti istituzionali in età laurenziana*, (Florence), Milan 1992.

P. Pirolo (ed.): *Lorenzo dopo Lorenzo. La fortuna storica di Lorenzo il Magnifico*, (Florence) Milan 1992.

A. Lenzuni (ed.): *All'ombra del Lauro. Documenti librari della cultura in età laurenziana*, (Florence), Milan 1992.

G. Rolfi - L. Sebregondi - P. Viti (ed.): *La Chiesa e la città di Firenze nel secolo XV*, (Florence), Milan 1992.

M. Gregori - A. Paolucci - C. Acidini Luchinat (ed.): *Maestri e botteghe. Pittura a Firenze alla fine del Quattrocento*, (Florence), Milan 1992.

F. Cardini (ed.): *Lorenzo il Magnifico*, Rome 1992.

P. Viti (ed.): 'Studi su Lorenzo dei Medici e il secolo XV', *Archivio Storico Italiano*, CL, fasc. II-IV, 1992.

Entertainment in Laurentian Florence
Paola Ventrone

Among the many myths surrounding Lorenzo de'Medici, the one regarding his patronage in the field of entertainment is surely one of the most deeply rooted, as it is linked to the untarnishable image of the prince who chose public spectacles as his *ad instrumentum regni* in the manner of the ancient patricians of Republican and Imperial Rome. Not even the continuous rethinking of Laurentian history has managed to cast any doubts on this aspect of his character, which in the year of celebration of the fifth centenary of his death, continues to surface in the speeches of politicians, journalists and sometimes even scholars.

This has arisen as a result of historical inaccuracies dating from princely times (particularly in Vasari's *Vite*), which give an idealized picture of life during the Laurentian era, seen as a "golden age" to which public appearances, in the presence of all the citizens, and Lorenzo's patronage contributed greatly. The myth of the golden age, which was then enhanced up by Leo X and cultivated by the Medici during the era of the Grand Dukes, was an attempt to constitute a "dynastic" line of continuity, intended to legitimize the family's rule in the eyes of the aristocracy and the citizens of Florence, after their return from exile.

Lorenzo's involvement in the organization of ceremonies and festivals actually takes on a rather different appearance when seen in the light of contemporary evidence. One realizes on reading through diaries, history books, archived material and eulogistic 15th century descriptions just how rare the occasions were when Lorenzo was actually responsible for putting on public entertainment. During his early years, he took part in equestrian games, as did all the younger generations of the aristocratic families. These games were quite firmly rooted in the tradition of Florentine festivities and greatly appreciated by its citizens. He really only became directly interested in city entertainment during the final period of his hegemony when, political life being relatively stable, he devised new attractions for the carnival and for the patronal festival of San Giovanni.

Equestrian games, jousts and tournaments in particular, were an accepted and important part of Florentine life during the 15th century. The great importance attached to courtly and chivalric outward appearances was an excuse for the upper and mercantile classes who controlled the city's trade to show off their wealth, offsetting the vulgarity of such gestures with the demonstration of their mastery of chivalric skills, such as their dexterity with weapons and the absolute control over their mounts. This image was compounded between the 14th and 15th centuries by ceremonies held in honour of visiting foreign dignitaries or to celebrate important political events affecting civilian life, such as peace, victories or alliances. During the visits of Pope Pius II and Galeazzo Maria Sforza in 1459, the city organized a series of ceremonies, each rooted in urban tradition, which included displays of every sort of "courtly ceremony" in vogue during the Quattrocento. There was a joust in the Piazza Santa Croce, a ball in the Mercato Nuovo, a hunt in the Piazza dei Signori and "armeggerie" in the Via Larga. "Armeggierie" were choreographed displays in which groups of men on horseback rode through the streets of the city in magnificent costumes to meet in one of the *piazze*, where they would show off their skills and the elegance of their accoutrements, standing up in their foreshortened stirrups and "splitting" their lances on the ground or against targets. The organization of these exercises was in the hands of the so-called "brigades": groups of youths, mainly from the ranks of the city's aristocracy, who got together especially for the occasion under the direction of a *signore* or *messere* who was responsible for all the formalities. The *messere* was therefore responsible for subsidising the festivities accompanying the display, the banquet and the ball, and the choice of uniforms and liveries. The uniform consisted of a short surcoat made of expensive material, on the right sleeve, and sometimes on the back or on the front, the brigade's emblem was embroidered, and a pair of striped multicolour narrow breeches or "stockings", also embroidered with the same emblem. Pictures of these emblems and of the late Gothic and courtly style of the clothes often appear in miniatures, on contemporary marriage plates or the front panels of bridal chests.

The ten year old Lorenzo acted as *messere* in the 1459 "armeggerie" – publicly presented as the future Medici heir during the event, and invested with spectacular and unprecedented glory. He was accompanied by the first known chariot bearing the "Triumph of Love", which was probably both a consequence and a cause of the ensuing currency subject enjoyed in figurative Florentine culture. The joust in the Piazza Santa Croce was a regular item on the city's festive calendar. It formed a regular part of the carnival and was sometimes held during the spring as well. Youths from the most prominent Florentine families took part as did foreign cavaliers and mercenary captains working for the Italian princes, whose presence was a testament to the state of political relations between the various states of the peninsula.

Apart from the purely technical side of the combat, the aspect that really attracted the audiences to the equestrian performances was the pomp and ceremony of the "demonstration", or prelude to the armed combat when the participants, accompanied by their ladies, the grooms and the burghers paraded through the streets of the city in their fabulous costumes, bearing highly expensive trophies. The many allusions to these events, in chronicles and diaries of the time often give details of the quality of the clothes and accessories, frequently in terms of their financial worth, before moving on to a description of the encounters and the names of the winners. For young Florentines in particular, taking part in the jousts meant that they had reached a milestone in terms of age, signifying that they were qualified to take public office. The twenty-year-old Lorenzo and, several years later, his brother Giuliano (in 1469 and 1475 respectively) had to go through this "rite of passage" and take their places in the field to show off their combative skills, each of them carrying off first prize.

The so-called "Medici Jousts" therefore became assimilated, quite naturally, into the chivalric tradition, as is evident from the matter-of-fact way in which they are described in the chronicles and diaries of witnesses. But if the dynamics of the performances and the preparations leading up to the jousts of 1469 and 1475 appeared to have been similar and indeed comparable (even bearing in mind the propagandist intentions underlying all such forms of entertainment), it has to be recognized that, at the planning stage, there was a huge cultural difference. The former was conceived in the Nordic manner, with the epic image of the brave cavalier prepared to fight for the love of his lady; whereas the latter bore all the hallmarks of Poliziano's strong character and the underlying traces of the Neoplatonist philosophy that translated Giuliano's combative trial into an initiation into the ethical responsibilities of maturity. These meanings, although not always evident to the average spectator, were always alluded to in the reviews Lorenzo commissioned from Luigi Pulci and Angelo Poliziano (*La Giostra* and *Le Stanze*), therefore remained confined to the restricted social *milieu* of the Medici intellectuals, without assuming the outward value of propagandist tools.

Towards the end of his life, after the very long series of festivals and public ceremonies organized in the wake of the Pazzi conspiracy of 1478, Lorenzo appeared to be becoming interested in the city's traditional spectacles. In fact the only definite information about city festivals known to have been organized and paid for by him dates from around this time: the *Sette trionfi dei sette pianeti* for the 1490 carnival, for which he also wrote the songs, and the *Trionfi di Paolo Emilio*, which was included in the celebrations for the feast day of *San Giovanni* in 1491. In both cases, Lorenzo's work was both innovative and conservative and it is hardly surprising, therefore, how completely indifferent the many Florentine

chroniclers of the time were – only one of them noted the representation of Paulus Aemilius' chariots in the patronal procession. Both pieces were conservative in the sense that they both centred on the use of the device of the triumphal car, which was quite common in the context of civic entertainment, and as regards his choice of theme – the seven planets of Ptolemy's sky and the figure of the Roman leader which derives from Plutarch – both had been reasonably common figurative images since the beginning of the century at least, in the engravings for Baccio Baldini's famous calendar, for example.

The innovative elements, on the other hand, consisted of the tangible three-dimensional nature of the subjects, which although well-known did not belong to either of the celebrations in which they appeared, and of Lorenzo's responsibility, not just as financial patron, but as originator and orchestrator of the theme itself. Lorenzo's intervention in the celebration of the patronal feast of John the Baptist introduces another, no less important, aspect of urban festivities: religion. *San Giovanni* was the most important city festival of the year because traditionally it served as an outward demonstration of the civic unity of the Florentines. The basic point of departure for the celebrations was a series of hierarchically ordered processions of citizens who, variously grouped under the ensigns of their companies or the associations to which they belonged (the *gonfaloni*, the guilds, the magistracies, the religious orders, the confraternities, the representatives of subject lands), each carried wax tributes or precious banners – the *palii* – as offerings to their patron saint.

Naturally other elements were introduced into the programmes during the Quattrocento, the greatest of these being the *edifizi* or religious floats on which the main events from the Old or New Testaments dealing with the redemption of man from the fall of the rebellious angels to the Day of Judgement were represented. The *edifizi* were pulled through the streets of Florence the day before the religious and civil festivities began. Lorenzo's Triumphs of Paulus Aemilius formed part of this stage of the celebrations, possibly as a temporary substitute for some of the traditional religious floats, sowing the seeds of classical culture with a representation of the triumphant hero of Republican Rome who had managed to bring a period of peace and prosperity to the citizens of Urbe. To the Florentines, or at least to those Florentines intellectually capable of discerning the meaning of the entertainment, the figure of the leader might well have struck them as a reflection of the sage and balanced governor who, without ever rising to the position of legitimate *Signore*, had guided their destinies, bringing glory and well-being to their city. Although *San Giovanni* remained the city's main celebration, other unconnected yet no less important religious events gradually began to be incorporated into the yearly festivities: the *Feast of the Annunciation*, the *Feast of the Ascension* and *Pentecost* were celebrated in some of the Oltrarno churches by three companies of *laudesi* patronized by the Medici.

The fame, even at a historiographic level, of these entertainments, and of the first two in particular is mostly due to the use of theatrical machinery, the so-called *ingegni* or *apparatus* that made the special effects possible. This was described at length by Vasari, who claimed that Brunelleschi invented it.

The *Feast of the Ascension* was celebrated annually in the church of the Carmine, of the Order of St Agnes, throughout the Quattrocento and beyond. The descriptions and accounts of the period tell of marvellous scenes full of feats of technical ingenuity and fantastic lighting and music, all of which appeared to improve from year to year. The apparatus basically consisted of two particular positions, the castle and the hill which were located on the ground – or rather at the point in the nave where the stage began and the spectators' area ended – and a celestial space, paradise, located between the roof trusses. The two areas were linked by the "nuvola", or cloud, a lifting device operated by brackets on which two real children dressed as angels stood, secured by iron clasps and bars. They were then lowered down to meet Jesus and accompany him on his journey up to meet the Father. The sky too was full of children dressed up as musical angels, who were surrounded, as was the cloud, by a multitude of painted angels of varying shapes and sizes, which resulted in the very rich figurative effect.

The apparatus used for the *Feast of the Annunciation* in the church of San Felice was almost identical to that used for the Ascension:

it too hinged on a vertical system of connection between the place designed as the empyrean, again located among the roof trusses, and the earth, which was on a box on the floor. The moment of greatest drama was when the Archangel Gabriel descended from heaven to the house of the Virgin. The major differences were in the adaptation of the apparatus to the differing requirements of the subject: the castle and the hill were replaced by the house of the Virgin, whilst the cloud assumed the typical almond shape of the "mandorla", which appears in many contemporary paintings. As well as the scenic apparatus, there were other, more ephemeral, decorations made of cheap materials such as painted *papier-maché* and wood, that were used to adorn the inside and the outside of the churches where the performances were being held.

Here too, as in all the above-mentioned types of entertainment, Lorenzo tended to be a respector of tradition, although has to be said that he was a member of at least one of the confraternities responsible for these productions (the Compagnia di Sant'Agnese). He sometimes came to the performances, but there is no record of his ever having been involved either on the production side or with the *mise-en-scène*.

We can therefore conclude that Lorenzo was a statesman who took an occasional interest in the entertainments and feast-day celebrations of his city, although there is no question of his involvement in terms of production. Lorenzo was always greatly mindful of the customs of the Florentine festive tradition, and he accorded them due respect. Such a well thought-out approach was typical of the city's illegitimate Signore, who was conscious that his position of power in the city depended on his formal respect for the Republican institutions and consequently also of their festive traditions.

Selected Bibliography

A. d'Ancona: *Origini del teatro italiano*, Turin 1891.

G. Volpi: *Le feste di Firenze del 1459, Notizie di un poemetto del secolo XV*, Pistoia 1902.

C. Guasti: *Le feste di San Giovanni Battista in Firenze descritte in prosa e in versi dai contemporanei*, Florence 1908.

A. Warburg: *Gesammelte Schriften*, H. von Bius (ed.), Leipzig-Berlin 1932.

A. Rochon: *La Jeunesse de Laurent de Médicis (1449-1478)*, Paris 1963.

N. Rubinstein: *The Government of Florence under The Medici (1434-1494)*, Oxford 1966.

Il luogo teatrale a Firenze by M. Febbri, E. Garbero Zorzi, Anna M. Petrioli Tofani, Exhibition Catalogue (Florence), Milan 1975.

L. Zorzi: *Il teatro e la città. Saggi sulla scena italiana* Turin 1977.

R.C. Trexler: *Public Life in Renaissance Florence*, New York 1980.

Nuovo corpus di sacre rappresentazioni fiorentine del Quattrocento, edited by Nerida Newbigin, Bologna 1983.

N. Rubinstein: *The Posthumous Image of Lorenzo de'Medici, in Oxford, China and Italy. Writings in Honour of Sir Harold Acton on his Eightieth Birthday*, E.P. Chaney-N. Ritchie (ed.), Oxford 1984.

M. Martelli: *Firenze, in Letteratura italiana. Storia e geografia*, II: *L'età moderna*, Turin 1988, pp. 25-201.

V. Rossi: *Il Quattrocento* (Milan 1933), *Updated* by R. Bessi, *Introduction* by M. Martelli, Padua 1992.

Le tems revient – il tempo si rinuova, P. Ventrone (ed.), Exhibition catalogue (Florence), Milan 1992.

P. Ventrone: *Gli araldi della commedia. Teatro a Firenze nel Rinascimento*, Pisa 1993.

P. Ventrone: *L'eccezione e la regola: le rappresentazioni del 1439 nella tradizione fiorentina delle feste di quartiere*, from *Firenze e il Concilio del 1439*, Conference Papers (Florence 29th November-2nd December 1989), edited by P. Viti, Florence 1993, pp. 409-435.

The Chivalric "Ludus" in Quattrocento Florence
Mario Scalini

In spite of Petrarch's withering statement that during the 14th century that chivalry suited the Florentines as much as "a saddle on a pig", his opinion was largely contradicted by the facts or at least by the great tradition of almost continuous jousts and tournaments throughout both centuries.

In reality Petrarch, the humanist, was alluding to the eminently practical and mercantile mind of the Florentines, who were undoubtedly more inclined towards the arts, and the figurative arts in particular, far removed from the influence of Mars. Chivalry, even when conferred by the Comune itself, was in fact a necessary requirement in 14th century Tuscany since the dignity it afforded – once one had tightened the knightly "cingolo" or belt around one's waist and fastened on the golden spurs – meant that one was now considered ready to take up public office and qualified to join the *podestà*. Florence was therefore a city in which existed *cavalieri "di popolo e comune"* or *"di Parte"* [Guelfa] so-called when their "finery" was paid for by the latter. Chivalry was indeed a political tool, a means of affirming the city's hegemony over its neighbours, but the theatrical importance attached to the combat was by no means secondary. These ritualistic fights generated a great deal of financial interest, but their appeal in terms of fashion and propaganda was even greater. As has been underlined elsewhere, the holding of jousts and tournaments within the feudal courts and the national states beyond the Alps, was a way of keeping public spirits high and exercising an undoubtedly bellicose yet useful social aristocracy, controlling the series of as it were "patron-and-client" relationships between the various dynasties. Within a free city-state, such as Florence, it is possible that such displays of dexterity and bravery might well have had different meanings, and the effect on the spectators, the commoners and even those of equal social standing must have varied considerably, in spite of the obvious parallels in behaviour between the local magnates' offspring and the Nordic knights. These cavalier "sports" had been being played out for some time throughout the Italian peninsula, and Petrarch records how, in Angevin Naples, they sometimes degenerated into very real battles. However, according to Dante, the jousts recorded as having continued to take place during the campaign that led to the Battle of Campaldino (1289) were not excessively violent.

It must have been hard for the practical Florentines to jeopardize the lives of their own sons without serious reasons of state and great precautions had to be taken to avoid major bloodshed. Gaetano Salvemini, who studied the development of knightly codes of honour in the city-state of Florence had produced a precious series of bibliographical and documentary references for the purposes of studying the problem of the combative celebration-drama in the Tuscan capital. The source material available to him, enabled him to draw conclusions within the context of his particular area of research. More recently, in the light of renewed interest in these particular forms of display in Tuscany, it has become obvious that more concrete and tangible facts are required. It is no longer enough to rely on a simple accumulation of data or an attempt to see events through the eyes of the diarists.

Researchers have been hampered in their search for the real essence and importance of each event by a total absence of critical appraisal of the primary source and a complete lack of understanding of the organizational methods and the defensive and offensive methods employed. They have been forced to study an overview which, though general, or what the historians call an "established" picture, immediately founders in the context of a single proven episode.

It is fair to say that in Florence, tournaments were much less frequent than jousts and there is a social and political reason for this, as mentioned above. Just as displays and demonstrations were required of the Florentine infantrymen and the crossbowmen, with the intention of creating an *esprit de corps* and a healthy public attitude towards weapons, the (military) cavalrymen were required to show off their dexterity once or twice a year. 14th century Florentine jousts started out as combative exercises rather than as entertainment, defensive weapons and "courtesy" offensive weapons (their lances had rounded tips) were used. The medieval system of heraldic recognition, using shields and horse-armour painted with familiar emblems so as to avoid confusion on the battlefield, meant that both noblemen and commoners could follow the fortunes of the combatants, even to the extent of being able to distinguish between two members of the same family, thanks to the different crests they wore on their head pieces. As the century wore on and the martial arts changed, so did the differing perceptions of war throughout the Italian peninsula, and the motives for these public displays of chivalry and indeed their execution underwent a subtle yet radical change. It would take too long to list all the changes which, incomprehensibly it seems, appear for the most part to have gone undetected, but a general essay such as this ought to mention that the advent of suits of polished steel armour, devoid of any heraldic devices had a considerable effect on jousting. In Florence, unlike most of the rest of Italy and Europe, the jousts were still held in "open fields", carrying on the ancient tradition of attempting to make the contests look like real battle skirmishes in spite of there only being two armed combatants at a time, kept apart by lengths of cloth sometimes held down by stakes, which formed "rings" and marked out the two "channels" or corridors from which they mounted their attacks, each taking aim at the other.

A contender's worth was directly related to the precision with which he managed to penetrate his opponent's armour (preferably aiming at the helmet) and combat continued almost to the bitter end, in accordance with a Mediterranean custom common also in Spain. Foreign noblemen and even true professionals, whose job frequently was to try and forestall major injury to this or that young participant, would be invited to take part in particularly important jousts – important because eminent scions of the oligarchic society were taking part. The contests themselves were not rigged, as has been suggested, partly because the mechanics of the event would not have allowed it, and because the judges would have been bound to notice, but mostly because it would have been glaringly obvious to the audience thus bringing shame and dishonour to any youth having had to resort to such subterfuge during his first public combat. The splendour of the surcoats or *giornee* (silk "cassocks" that the contestants wore so as to be distinguishable on that occasion, i.e. on that specific day) alone was not enough to satiate the chroniclers, for even though they were impressed by the ostentation of some of the participants (in 1467, for example, Benedetto Salutati commissioned embroideries and enamels from the Pollaiolo brothers' workshop for his own costume and for his horse's harness and for his retinue), they never neglected to record the name of the winners and which of the participants had behaved bravely during the displays.

As a first trial almost as an initiation into public life for the eighteen-year-old youths, these jousts were moments of singular importance, judging by the records of their delight at their prowess and of the daring feats of the youngest of them. These feats of daring or "*bagordi*" were another demonstration of personal dexterity in which one of the youths, generally accompanied by a group of friends, would charge his horse towards one of the walls of the *palazzo* of a young lady, shying away at the very last minute yet still managing to break his spear against the wall. This was a true demonstration of daring and equestrian skill and this particular display of armsmanship became part of a courting ritual by dint of the all too obvious erotic symbolism attached to the spear and the stone wall. These displays of youthful bravery also served as forewarnings of the dangers these young men might have to face as adults, when not only would they have to show off their skills to the parents of their intended brides but would also have to make their

mark as potential suitors. It was for this reason that the youths who took part in the *bagordi* would be dressed in allusive colours such as green and in a rather ostentatiously monied way.

The "armeggerie" were similar in many ways, but the young men who took part in them were not trying to impress future brides (there are brief notes of many of these, kept by contemporaries) but the most significant tournament was the one in which Lorenzo de' Medici took part, in front of the family home in the Via Larga in 1459. The idea was to charge at the figure of a young man covered from head to foot in shiny or "polished" armour, mounted on a wooden stand in the middle of the road. For this event Piero's son wore a "noble and handsome shield on his chest" to distinguish him from the other participants and which we can visualize as having been a plate with an opening, or rather a concave rectangular metal shield with a deep groove on the same side as the spear, enabling this to be positioned so as to ensure greater precision of aim. We do not know whether the shield was painted or whether it was covered with precious material, embroidered or encrusted with jewels, or even if it was decorated with lozenges like the ones intended simply for display or for the decoration of noblemen's chapels and houses. It is likely, however, to have been in keeping with the importance of Lorenzo's family in spite of his tender age, given the unusual description of it as being "noble". The joust of 1469 was quite a different matter. I have already pointed out that the jousts were not always the same, and precise instructions (which stated quite definitively which combative appartenances, such as armour etc., were to be used, as well as the precise rules to be followed so as to avoid being disqualified or sent off) were issued each time. It is also worth mentioning that deep significance was attached to the different sorts of equipment and to any variation in the rules, a significance that would now only be obvious to experts in the field of 15th century symbolism and materials.

Thanks to the *Ricordo d'una giostra fatta a Firenze al dì 7 febbraio 1468 sulla piazza di Santa Croce ...*, published by Fanfani (in *Il Borghini*) in 1864, we have an extremely detailed picture of the event itself and of its festal background, in spite of an almost total absence of relevant archaeological data. During the extremely splendid cavalcade or "exhibition", Lorenzo was at the head of a procession that must have looked much like the one in Jacopo Bellini's portrait of Borso d'Este in the British Museum in London (sketchbook ff. 53 v. – 54) with an armed cavalcade and "*1 Paggio a cavallo vestito d'un gonnellino di velluto bianco e pagonazzo, con una berretta in capo di detto drappo. Portava in mano 1 stendardo di taffettà bianco e pagonazzo cor uno sole nella sommità e sottovi un arco baleno, e nel mezzo di detto stendardo v'era una dama ritta su un prato vestita di drappo alessandrino ricamato a fiori d'oro e d'ariento, e muovesi d'in sul campo pagonazzo uno ceppo d'alloro con più rami secchi, e nel mezzo uno ramo verde che si distendeva fino nel campo bianco, e pel campo pagonazzo e seminato di rami d'alloro secco. 1a Coverta al detto sino in terra di taffettà bianco e pagonazzo, con guazzeroni intorno, e frangiata a sua divisa".*

The "*divisa*" (device) featured the three colours chosen by Lorenzo: white, crimson and green, as did the *mazzocchi* and the plumes adorning the helmets, which had (typically Italian) T-shaped facial openings. These were worn by a hundred pages, armed with the standard fixed weapons with bronze ferrules, like the ones the King of England had purchased through the Peruzzi family to send from Florence. This part of the procession testified to both the city and the family's military and bellicose power and Giuliano, who was accompanying his brother, showed off a precious set of horse-armour, presented as a token of friendship by the Duke of Milan, with an embossed steel headpiece in the shape of a dragon. Lorenzo's "giornea", the short surcoat that combattants wore over their armour, was embroidered with fresh and dried roses, according to his chronicler, as was his horse's trappings, set with a great many precious jewels. For the tournament itself, Piero's son changed to what was ostensibly a simpler livery. In reality it was similar to that of the King of France, with three gold fleurs-de-lys on an azure background in recognition of the honour bestowed on his father – the right to incorporate the royal arms of France into the Medici family crest in perpetuity. As if to underline this reference to the family's international connections, the young cavalier had chosen a set of armour identical to that favoured by the Burgundian and Franco-Flemish courts – the detailed descriptions of the parts of the armour where his opponents' blows fell have been compared with that worn by the other participants and with what remains of Philip the Fair's jousting armour. These and other details have furnished enough information to conjure up a reasonable picture of these costumes and armour, graphically as well as mentally, which in some cases can be considered to be quite accurate.

When it was Giuliano's turn to take the field and show off his skills, on 27th January 1475, his jousting armour was made by a craftsman from the famous Milanese workshop of Antonio Missaglia, who was the undisputed European market leader, and only his shield, decorated with a Gorgon's head set with pearls thought possibly the work either of the Pollaiolo workshop or of Verrocchio, lent an extravagant and sumptuous touch to his appearance. It was a sophisticated piece of ostentation which disintegrated, blow by blow during the contest, almost as a premonition of a splendour that having reached such dizzy heights could only hope for a slow but splendid decline.

Selected Bibliography

M. Scalini: *The Weapons of Lorenzo de' Medici*, in *Art, Arms and Armour*, I, Chiasso 1979, pp. 13-29.

La Società in costume, giostre e tornei nell'Italia di Antico Regime, Foligno 1986.

M. Scalini: *Il Saracino e gli spettacoli cavallereschi nella Toscana granducale*, Florence 1987.

Il sabato di San Barnaba. La battaglia di Campaldino, Milan 1989.

La civiltà del torneo (sec. XII-XVII), Narni 1990.

M. Scalini: *L'armatura fiorentina del Quattrocento e la produzione d'armi in Toscana*, in *Guerra e guerrieri nella Toscana del Rinascimento*, Florence-Pisa 1990, pp. 83-126.

F. Quinterio: *La festa sacra e profana*, in

'Per bellezza, per studio, per piacere'. *Lorenzo il Magnifico e gli spazi dell'arte*, Florence 1991, pp. 79-98.

M. Scalini: *Divise e livree, araldica quotidiana*, in *Leoni vermigli e candidi unicorni*, Prato 1992, pp. 49-65.

M. Scalini: *Il "ludus" equestre nell'età laurenziana*, in *Le Tems revient. Il tempo si rinuova, feste e spettacoli nella Firenze di Lorenzo il Magnifico*, Florence 1992, pp. 75-102.

L. Ricciardi: *Col Senno col tesoro e colla lancia. Riti e giochi cavallereschi nella Firenze del Magnifico Lorenzo*, Florence 1992.

M. Scalini: *Armature ad Urbino: l'opera di Paolo Ucello e Piero*, in *Piero e Urbino, Piero e le corti rinascimentali*, Venice 1992, pp. 179-187.

M. Scalini: *Lorenzo e le armi*, in *Lorenzo il Magnifico*, Rome 1992, pp. 257-272.

Francesco D'Antonio
**Organ Shutters Representing
Singing Angels with Saint Matthew
and Saint John**
1492
Tempera on panel; 206 x 119 cm;
206 x 110 cm
Florence, Accademia del Disegno
(on loan from the Gallerie
Fiorentine)

Beato Angelico
Crucifixion
c 1435
Parchment; 340 x 220 mm;
Tempera and gold
Florence, Monastero di Santa Trinita

Paolo Uccello (attr.)
The Road to Perfection
1460s
Oil on canvas; 81 x 111 cm
Florence, Galleria dell'Accademia
(Inv. no. 5381)

Unknown 15th-century Master
The Agony of Savonarola
Wooden panel; 100 x 115 cm
Florence, Museo di San Marco

Florentine Goldsmith
Processional Cross
early 15th century
Cast bronze, chased, fretworked
and gilded; 49.5 x 28.3 cm
Florence, Church of Santa Maria
nella Badia Fiorentina

Florentine workshop
Incense-Boat
first quarter 15th century
Engraved and cast copper; 7 x 17 cm
Tignano (Barberino Val d'Elsa),
Church of San Romolo

Florentine workshop
Medicean Chasuble
first quarter 16th century
113 x 73 cm
Florence, Church of SS. Annunziata
(Work without illustration)

Vallombrosian Cape
Velvet with Medici crest,
15th century
210 x 100 cm
Florence, Museo degli Argenti
(Inv. Tessuti Antichi no. 851)

Tuscan workshop
Cushion
before 1477
Wool and silk; 26 x 26.5 x 27 x 29
cm, h. 2.5 cm
Impruneta, Museo del Tesoro della
Basilica di Santa Maria

Tuscan workshop
Thurible
mid-15th century
Silver-plated, embossed and engraved;
h. 27 cm
Pistoia, Museo Diocesano

Florentine workshop
Chalice, second half 15th century
Gilded copper, embossed, chiselled
and engraved; 19 cm h.
Certaldo, Church of San Donato

Giusto da Firenze (attr.)
Chalice
c 1480
Embossed, chiselled and engraved
silver, partially gilded; 31 x 13.7 cm
Florence, Church of Sant'Ambrogio

Giovanni di Stoldo Nutini (attr.)
Peace
1455
Embossed and chased silver (internal plaque); cast, engraved silver, partly gilded (frame); 20 x 14.5 x 5.5 cm
Florence, Cattedrale di Santa Maria del Fiore

Florentine Goldsmith and Illuminator
Peace
late 15th century
Gold-plated silver, translucent
enamel; illumination on parchment;
19 x 13 cm
Florence, Church of San Michele
and San Salvi

Antonio di Salvi
**Reliquary of San Gordiano
and Other Saints**
1490-1491
Embossed, chiselled, engraved
and gold-plated copper; cast silver,
embossed, chiselled and fretworked;
translucent enamel; niello; 57 x 28 x
14 cm
Florence, Church of Santa Maria
nella Badia Fiorentina

The Entertainment

Giovanni di Ser Giovanni, known
as Lo Scheggia
**The Marriage of Lionora de' Bardi
and Ippolito Buondelmonti**
mid-15th century
Front panel of chest, tempera
on wooden panel; 42 x 157 cm
Collection of Alberto Bruschi
di Grassina

Giovanni di Ser Giovanni, known
as Lo Scheggia
The Game of Civettino
mid-15th century
Tempera on wooden panel;
59 cm diameter
Florence, Museo di Palazzo
Davanzati (Inv. 1890 no. 488)

FRANCISCI PETRARCE TRIVM
PHORVM SEX LIBER VNICVS FELI
CITER INCIPIT.
VALE QVI LEGERIS.

Eltempo che rinuoua
imie fofpiri
Per ladolce memoria
di quel giorno
Che fu principio a fi lu
ohi martiri.

Francesco Petrarch
Triumphs and Rhymes
Florence, c 1450-1460
Parchment; 248 x 170 mm;
216 leaves; modern numbering
Decorated with historical scenes
on reverse of 1, 17, 22, 34, 43, 47,
corresponding to the Triumphs,
mainly the work of Giovanni
Varnucci, probably assisted by his
brother Bartolomeo. Bound in green
silk on board; embossed gilt edge
Biblioteca Nazionale Centrale
di Firenze, Palat. 192

15th Century Umbrian School
Candelabras in the Form of Angels,
Papier-Maché on Wood; 45.5 cm h.
Rome, Museo di Palazzo Venezia
(Inv. no. 7590)

Unknown Tuscan Sculptor
Roundel with Monogram of Saint Bernardino
last quarter 15th century
Gilt papier-maché; 68 cm diameter
Florence, Museo Stibbert
(Inv. no. 334)

Medicean Device
Florence, second half 15th century
Two carved wood panels; 47 x 47 cm
Florence, Bardini Legacy
(Inv. 11507)

**Ornamental Border with Heraldic
Devices**
Florence, c 1466
Carved wood; 39 x 31 cm each crest
Florence, Bardini Legacy
(Inv. 11833)

**Square of Decorative Edging with
Medici Crest**
Florence, second half 15th century
Lampas; 29 x 29 cm
Florence, Bardini Legacy no. 8121
(no. 161)

Unknown Florentine Goldsmith
Necklace Pendant
c 1470-1480
Silver, white and green enamel, gold
and precious stones; 3.5 x 2.5 cm
Private Collection

The Chilvaric Ludus

Workshop of Antonio del Pollaiolo;
Unknown 17th century Goldsmith;
Unknown 19th century Goldsmith
**Emblem in the Form of an Eagle
on Top of Ceremonial Helmet**,
Florence
c 1450-1460
Embossed, engraved and gold-plated
copper, steel, velvet and gilt bronze;
20 cm (emblem), 46 cm (total)
Florence, Museo Stibbert
(Inv. no. 16206)

Florentine workshop
Helmet
late 15th century
Iron
Florence, Museo Nazionale
del Bargello (Inv. Armi 1435 M)

Antonio Pollaiolo
**Archangel Michael Slaying
the Dragon**
1460-1470
Tempera on canvas; 175 x 116 cm
Florence, Museo Bardini (Inv. 776)

Master IO.F.F. (Francesco Furnio,
attr.)
Plaque
(possibly originally a helmet
ornament) showing the Judgement of
Paris, perhaps belonging to Lorenzo
de' Medici, Bologna, before 1492
Engraved and gilded bronze, 5.5 cm
Private Collection
(Work without illustration)

**Reconstructions of the Costumes
and Armaments for Lorenzo's
Jousting Tournament of 1469**
Pen drawings, with watercolour, gold
and silver; models in cast lead,
engraved and painted
Scale, respectively 1:15, 1:30

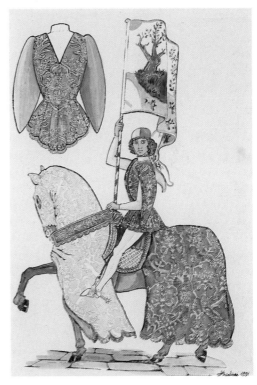

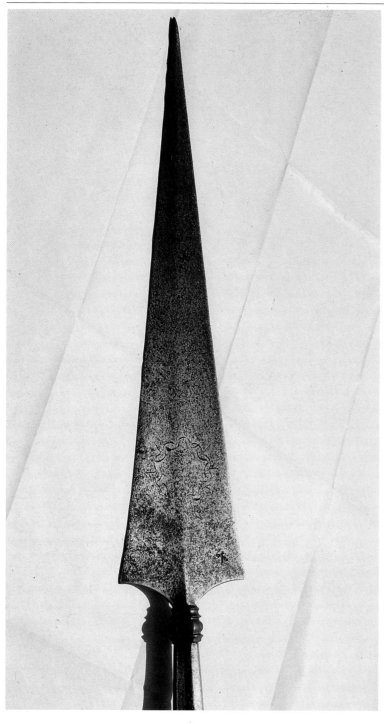

Florentine workshop
Spit
c 1480-1490
Steel, bronze and wood (modern);
614 mm long
Florence, Museo Stibbert
(Inv. no. 2797)

Maestro Tonino
Falchion
second half 15th century
Steel and wood (modern); 180 cm
Cortona, Museo dell'Accademia
Etrusca
(Inv. T.B. 473/1)

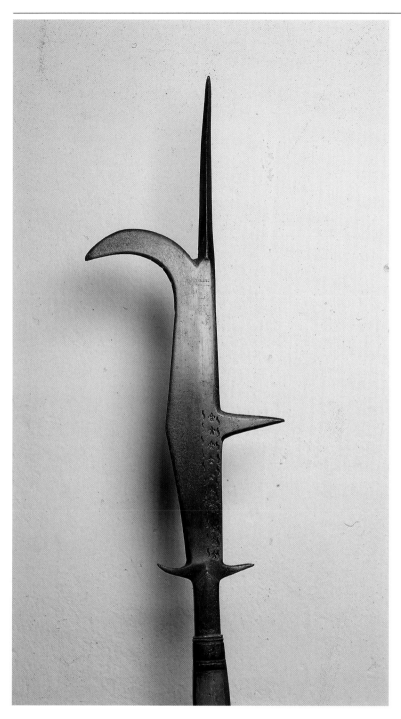 

Lance Tip
Florence, second half 15th century
Steel, bronze and wood (modern);
180 cm
Cortona, Museo dell'Accademia
Etrusca
(Inv. T.B. 473/3)

Lance Tip
Florence, early 16th century
Steel and wood (modern);
180 cm
Cortona, Museo dell'Accademia
Etrusca
(Inv. T.B. 473/2)

The Arts

Arts in the Workshops during the Laurentian Age
Cristina Acidini Luchinat

The measure of success of all the works of art, the archaeological pieces, the *objets d'art* and all the historical items displayed in the Laurentian exhibitions of 1992 depended on the visitors managing to keep a mental picture of them after leaving the exhibitions, as they followed the celebratory itinerary through the city and the territory and the museums, churches, palaces and villas, which enabled them to place the works and objects in a historical perspective within the context for which they were intended. Within limits it is even possible to integrate and contextualize the exhibits we have brought to London, if our exhibition can be taken as being complementary with the collections of the Victoria & Albert Museum, the National Gallery and the Courtauld Institute. These collections and institutions were greatly expanded during the last century when the vogue for collecting was at its height, with the addition of works from the "major" and "minor" arts on which our knowledge and culture of the Florentine Renaissance is based. A visit to the National Gallery to see Pollaiolo and Botticelli's masterpieces is imperative, as is a visit to the Victoria & Albert Museum where there are a great many Florentine reliefs in the sculpture galleries, amongst which is the terracotta relief of the *Madonna and Child with St John* which, when we were planning the Florentine exhibition "Maestri e botteghe. Pittura a Firenze alla fine del Quattrocento" seemed to be a perfect example of the concept of well thought-out and co-ordinated teamwork amongst artists. The relief was worked in the Da Maiano workshop and is thought to have been coloured by Bartolommeo di Giovanni, a versatile painter from Ghirlandaio's circle, and author of the *Trinity with Two Angels* in the lunette above.

The pilgrim who is inspired by an exhibition such as this, dedicated to the arts of the Laurentian age, will have a very long and emotional journey through the galleries of the London museums in his attempt to reconcile Lorenzo, the man, with the home of his fathers in the Via Larga. He will see Paolo Uccello's *Battle of San Romano* in the National Gallery, with Niccolò da Tolentino at the head of the Florentine troops, which Lorenzo hung in his summer room on the ground floor – looking out over the peaceful walled garden – together with the other two *Battles* now in the Uffizi and the Louvre, all perhaps rather weighty works inherited from his grandfather Cosimo. Also in the National Gallery are Filippo Lippi's two lunettes of the *Annunciation* and the *Seven Saints*, thought to have come from one of the barrel vaulted rooms in the Medici palace. According to Davies, the seven are patron saints of various family members and the picture alludes to an awaited birth, which would have been Lorenzo's in 1449. In the Victoria & Albert

Museum there are Della Robbia's splendid glazed terracotta roundels of the twelve *Months*, which came from the barrel vaulted ceiling above the precious *studiolo* where Piero, Lorenzo's father, kept jewels, manuscripts and other treasures; there is also Donatello's *Ascension*, which hung in Lorenzo's room on the first floor. Apart from these works, which are definitive examples of Medici purchasing power, there are a multitude of other pieces in the same collections and institutions which help to give a better understanding of the period in question, thanks to the passion for collecting fine things and the highly refined concept of art as a whole that was the mark of the sensitivity and culture of the late 19th century in England.

The figurative and ornamental works of the Florentine Quattrocento – and of the highly productive later years in particular, when there was an extraordinary level of artistic output both in terms of quantity and quality – seemed to respond to an intimate psychological and stylistic need. The extraordinary affair of one of the most famous anglo-Florentines, Herbert Horne, was sparked off by the poetic and artistic experience of the Pre-Raphaelites, of William Morris and Arthur Mackmurdo (who courageously founded the Century Guild in 1882), by the writing of Walter Pater and John Ruskin and the work of Rossetti and Burne-Jones. Horne went to Florence in 1895 to spend a few weeks writing a book on Alessandro Filipepi, otherwise known as Botticelli, and remained there, captivated, until his death. He bought and restored the Palazzo Corsi in the Via de'Benci and started a collection, now housed in the museum which bears his name. His choice of objects reflects a sensitivity of taste nurtured within the bosom of English culture, and it was only in 1908 that his editor, a Mr Hill, managed to wrest the monograph on Botticelli out of his hands, which continues to be one of the definitive works of scientific criticism of the artist to this day.

Botticelli became and indeed remains an international legend (which contributed in no small way to Florence's reputation as a capital of art). But this century has seen the publication of a vast quantity of Renaissance studies which all attest to the fact that there were a myriad minor artists working alongside the great masters in Florence and in the territory, who built up a network of productive relationships both amongst themselves and between the major artists, in itself a major cultural achievement in Florence during the second half of the Quattrocento.

The main concept behind the exhibition entitled "Maestri e botteghe" (Masters and Workshops) held in 1992, was an attempt to retrieve the major links in this network, through literary research and the identification of relevant works of art. This was not an attempt to glorify the major artists who were already well known, rather a search for precise information about the complexity and multiplicity of the structuring of their work and an attempt to identify and evaluate works of the less famous or obscure artists who were active within the varied and dynamic framework of the Renaissance art industry.

Andrea del Verrocchio enjoyed a virtually unchallenged position of supremacy, at least as regards the variety of artwork available from his large, well-organised and prestigious workshop. This was patronized by the Medici family and by Lorenzo in particular who, with his younger brother Giuliano, gave his first important artistic commission there: this was the porphyry and bronze sepulchre for his father Piero, who died in 1469 (the remains of his uncle Giovanni, who died six years earlier, were also entombed there) in the Old Sacristy in the church of San Lorenzo of which the family were patrons. The porphyry sarcophagus was set against the wall that divides the Sacristy and the chapel of St Cosma and St Damian or the chapel of the Blessed Sacrament, also patronized by the Medici, in 1472. It is set beneath a vault criss-crossed with bronze tracery which has all the majesty of the barrel vault of a Roman triumphal arch and is decorated with finely wrought bronze and elegant inscriptions carved in antique lapidary letters. Quite apart from the excellence of the execution, the tomb is a fine example of the determination and discernment of the young clients. In his choice of Verrocchio, Lorenzo was carrying on a family tradition: Verrocchio, who was primarily a goldsmith and sculptor, had been responsible for the restoration and installation of the antiques in the palace in the Via Larga and had been commissioned to produce the decorations for the fountains in the Medici gardens, amongst other things. Lorenzo's patronage ensured that Verrocchio's commissions became increasingly prestigious (the monumental bronze group of the *Incredulity of St Thomas* in the shrine made for the Tribunal of Six of the Mercanzia, restored and exhibited in 1992 is one example, as is the hollow copper ball on the cupola of the Duomo). His workshop seethed with all sorts of different activities: pictures on panels and canvas banners, marble and bronze sculpture, goldsmithery and embroidery designs. Andrea was too busy to handle everything himself but was responsible for the inspiration and general planning of the works, leaving their execution to his assistants, as was the custom in all workshops. Thus we can detect the hands of both Botticelli and Leonardo, briefly working together as young pupils, in the *Baptism of Christ* executed for the church of San Salvi (now in the Galleria degli

Uffizi); a monumental work which was then copied by one of Verrocchio's assistants and friends, Lorenzo di Credi, for the Compagnia dello Scalzo (1490-95, now in the church of San Domenico at Fiesole).

Apart from these three great masters, other talented and versatile artists passed through Verrocchio's workshop: among them, according to Vasari, was the young Perugino, whose Florentine output included a problematic group of paintings amongst which, according to Federico Zeri, is the *Madonna with Child in her Lap Flanked by Two Angels* in the National Gallery. Two other less famous artists, Biagio d'Antonio and Francesco Botticini both worked with Verrocchio for set periods.

Biagio was best known later as one of Ghirlandaio's circle, but was temporarily influenced by Verrocchio's style, making sophisticated foreshortened heads typical of the master, as did the young Leonardo. Botticini, whose son Raffaello followed in his footsteps, painted the panel of the *Archangel Raphael with Tobias*, which is in the exhibition and was originally in the Badia Fiorentina but now kept in the Sacristy at the Duomo. The subject was a favourite among the merchants with young sons, in the hope that the Archangel would watch over their first journeyings and their first encounters, and the iconography was popular in Florence at that time. In this painting, the very blond youth kneeling bottom left is Agnolo Doni, thought to have been about ten when the panel was painted, circa 1484-85. Raphael's portrait of the same sitter, now adult and newly wed is in the Palatine Gallery. Botticini's apprenticeship in Verrocchio's workshop taught him – apart from the fluid lines of movement and drapery of his figures, reminiscent in part of Botticelli – the goldsmith's precise attention to detail with regard to materials, jewels and other ornaments, and his instinctive and calligraphic brushwork renders them almost lifelike, as can be seen in his masterpiece, the *Tabernacle of St Sebastian* in the Museo della Collegiata in Empoli.

Jacopo del Sellaio's delicate paintings are pleasantly imitative of Botticelli's slightly sophisticated artistic vocabulary. Although much taken with the sinuous grace of the master's figures, he was held back by his own limitations and his performance was variable. His diptych of the *Annunciation* depicts a motionless and ponderous Virgin, while the slim garlanded adolescent figure of the *Angel of the Annunciation* rises up through the narrow panel from an undulating swirl of drapes.

Moving on to Botticelli himself, there is a painting in the exhibition which dates from sometime during the last ten years of his life, quite possibly around 1495. This was a tempestuous and momentous year which saw the arrival of Charles VIII, signalling an abrupt end to the Laurentian era, the exiling of Piero de' Medici in 1494 and Savonarola's disappearance from the scene, already under threat of being burnt at the stake by the Romans in 1496. The *Madonna del Roseto* from the Palatine Gallery in the Palazzo Pitti, whose provenance is unknown, is an affecting work, depicting the Madonna placing the Infant Jesus into the arms of St John, against a background of rose bushes. For a long time this was considered to have been studio-work, but after a considerable quantity of over painting, retouching and different varnishes was removed during restoration, the unquestionably high quality of the picture led it to be attributed to Botticelli himself, and the cold yet splendid use of the paint and the wealth of fine details are a fundamental part of the master's personal artistic vocabulary. In spite of the serenity of the theme, the Madonna's abandoned pose and the tragic intensity of the embrace of the two boys exude a definite sense of foreboding, and anticipate later works by Botticelli: the *Mystic Nativity* in the National Gallery, for example.

The disconnected and dramatic sequence of gestures was an early example of Botticelli's later predilection for figures surprised in positions of restless energy, in the grip of overwhelming emotions such as pain or stupor: the four *Miracles of St Zenobius* in the Metropolitan Museum in New York, dating from the glorious period 1495-1500, or the pair of painted headboards the *Stories of Virginia* (in the Accademia Carrara in Bergamo) and the *Stories of Lucretia* (in the Isabel Stewart Gardner Museum in Boston) circa 1499-1500 are examples of this.

The picture from the Palatine Gallery gives us an opportunity to concentrate on one of the important practices common to the artistic workshops of the 15th century, namely the repeated use not just of the same composition, but of the same full-size drawing ("cartoon") worked out by the master and passed on to his assistants who then produced copies and variations. There is in fact a reversed replica of the Pitti *Madonna*, exactly the same size but of inferior quality, in the Barber Institute in Birmingham. All the evidence points to its having been worked from Botticelli's drawing by one of his immediate circle of artists.

An established system of exchange of drawings both within the workshops and between them meant that there were many such instances of re-use and distribution of particularly fine examples within the Florentine artistic community during the second half of the Quattrocento, even as regards painting and sculpture. An example of this is the very stiff painted ancon of the *Adoration with St John* in the Museo Bardini in Florence, by a follower of Filippo Lippi and Pesellino known as the Pseudo Pier Francesco Fiorentino. The small ancon is remarkable for its antique carved and gilded frame and depicts a group of three figures copied from the central part of the altarpiece with the same subject that Lippi made for the Cappella dei Magi in the Medici Palace, now in the Dahlem Museen.

Another full copy was produced in Lippi's workshop and later set on the Medici altar in place of the original. The subject was repeated several times by the same painter and by others, with many variations, presumably because of its suitability as a domestic icon. In this picture the subject is finely executed, particularly in the delicate and extremely detailed painting of the rose bushes (which take the place of the more usual and arcaic gold background). Pictures for domestic use, both sacred and secular (usually of small format), as well as pieces of furniture painted with figures and historical scenes decorated the houses of upper middle class families in varying degrees of luxury. The decoration of the Medici homes was in a great and admirable class of its own – the decoration of the palace Michelozzo built for Cosimo for example, or the "old family home" which was used by Pierfrancesco's branch of the family – where, among the furnishings, antiques and sculptures, there were paintings by great masters such as Fra Angelico, Uccello, Filippo Lippi and Botticelli. Even in the houses and palaces belonging to other wealthy Florentine families the rooms, particularly those used for entertaining and the bedrooms, contained furniture and figurative works that the artistic industry of the time produced in massive quantities.

A beautiful wood frame from the Museo Davanzati is also exhibited, as a sample of Quattrocento craftmanship.

The coffer or nuptial chest, better known as the bridal chest or cassone, was a basic piece of furniture which was placed in the bedroom of the newly weds on the occasion of their marriage, often part of the dowry and frequently lined and figured (the exhibition contains the cassone with the *Marriage of Lionora de' Bardi* by Scheggia from the Bruschi collection). The marriage plates, which held sweetmeats for the puerpera, were no less ornate and the plate decorated by Scheggia and presented to Lucrezia Tornabuoni Medici on the occasion of Lorenzo's birth in 1449 (New York Historical Society) is deservedly famous. This carried a scene, which proved to be prophetic as well as auspicious, of a Petrarchesque *Triumph of Fame*. The rooms might well have been decorated with large paintings inserted into complicated wooden frames which acted as "back rests" against the wall, or sometimes into "day beds" which were large chests with armrests and backs used for short rests during the day. Smaller pictures were hung directly on the walls and usually depicted religious scenes. The favourite themes were happy and familiar ones like the *Adoration* or the *Madonna del Latte*, although there were plenty of paintings of painful and severe devotion, like *Christ Suffering* and the *Crucifixion*. Historical and mythological subjects were used mostly for coffers and back rests, although there are many examples of smaller works.

The cycle of works dedicated to the story of Nebuchadnezzar and Daniel, though biblical in origin, were apposite and worldly complements to their contemporary surroundings. Four small panels have been discovered (possibly from a now dismantled set of furniture): here we have *Nebuchadnezzar Interrogating Daniel and his Companions* from the Bruschi Collection, ideally accompanied by the scenes of *The Treasure of the Temple of Jerusalem brought to the Temple of Apollo* and *Daniel Explaining Nebuchadnezzar's Dream* (Georgia, Atlanta Museum, Kress Collection), and *The Dream* (formerly Florence coll. Landau Finlay). The author of the series, known as the "Master of the *Apollini Sacrum*" from the name-piece in Atlanta, has been definitively identified as the Master of Marradi, who although of secondary importance was an artist of character. He generally worked in peripheral cities and was in fact separated from Florence by a range of fairly impassable mountains. During the final years of the 15th century, although geographically distanced, the master managed to combine his own basic archaism with novel ideas gleaned from the works of artists such as Botticelli and Ghirlandaio, as can be seen by the frontal disposition of his figures and the use of his own personal, unorthodox perspectival logic.

There was no shortage of archaic painters in the variegated artistic panorama of Florence in the Quattrocento, who were all reasonably *au fait* with the modern representational techniques such as the disposition of masses, perspective and plays of light, although they continued to rely on the traditional splendour of gold and occasionally fell back on very outmoded techniques (lack of proportion, for example, between the large figure of a Saint and the small praying figure). Benozzo Gozzoli was one of them, in certain aspects of his work. He was Fra Angelico's greatest assistant and was chosen by Cosimo and Piero de' Medici to paint the frescoes of the *Procession of the Magi* and *The Adoring Angels* (1459) in the chapel of the Medici Palace. They are frescoes of extraordinary and fabulous splendour that combine perspective and an almost Flemish limpid clarity of vision with the analytical precision of the goldsmith and illustrator, particularly as regards the decorations which are lavishly embellished with gold. Following this was the notable series of professional successes from the family workshop of Neri di Bicci, son and pupil of Bicci di Lorenzo. During the 1470s Neri brought his own rigid enamelled style to painted panels, that seemed to belong to a sort of hieratic decorativism with the hardness of their design and the compact splendour of their gold backgrounds. Neri painted the *Croce Astile* from the Museo Bandini at Fiesole near Florence, probably executed for the Benedictine Convent of Sant'Apollonia, shortly after 1475. The crucifix is intended to be borne aloft during solemn processions and is painted on both sides, with *Christus Triumphans* with St Benedict, St Apollonia and St Francis on one side, and *Christus Patiens* with God the Father, the Virgin Mary and SS John the Evangelist and Mary Magdalene on the other. With its polylobe outline bristling with turned finials (in the manner of metallic crosses of the period), richly gilded and finely painted, the Fiesole cross is a superb example of ecclesiastical ornamentation, combining artistic elements with precious materials and impeccable craftsmanship.

Among the other artists whose style was arcaicised and sometimes naive, was the painter known as the Master of the Johnson Nativity, whom recent research has now identified as Domenico di Zanobi, associate of the more famous Domenico di Michelino. One of his paintings, which is remarkable for its subject matter rather than its technique (hard and naive), was produced in the church of Santo Spirito, designed by Brunelleschi, which was an extraordinary hive of artistic activity during the Florentine Renaissance. The painted panels and altar frontals commissioned by the great Oltrarno families are still to be found in the rich clear spaces of the chapels. The painted panel in the exhibition, painted thanks to a bequest from Pietro Velluti in approximately 1475-76, shows a rather folksy *Madonna del Soccorso* who, in front of a terrified mother, is using a stick to chase away the devil who is endeavouring to possess the soul of her son. The subject is unusual in Florence, though common in the Marche and in Umbria, and appears to refer to a miracle performed by the Virgin Mary, who saved a child conceived in sin during the penitential period of Holy Week. The painting also contains a warning to all parents against the risks of tardy baptism. The frontal featuring the tondo of the *Descent of the Holy Spirit* with the Biliotti family, on an imitation cloth embroidered with haloed doves, by an unknown artist also comes from Santo Spirito. These painted altarpieces replaced the cloth ones, but had the same function of beautifying the front of altars; there used to be many of them but now they are few, although there are at least ten in Santo Spirito.

If it is true to say, therefore, as is generally held, that Florentine art during the second half of the 15th century is typified by Botticelli's style and its influence on his contemporaries, it is no less true to say, as specialist studies have revealed, that the enormous quantity of works of art and meticulous craftsmanship allowed all its exponents to express themselves in a multitude of ways and to prosper under the auspices of their very varied patrons. It is difficult to categorize and define Lorenzo de' Medici's role as client within this artistic spectrum for it was, as Gombrich defines perfectly, "elusive". "It comes as a shock of suprise to realise how few works of art there are in existence which can be proved to have been commissioned by Lorenzo".

A vast amount of published and unpublished research was carried out between the Florentine exhibition of 1949, which was dedicated to art in the Laurentian age, during the fifth centenary of Lorenzo's birth, and the 1992 exhibitions, which stressed Lorenzo's passion for collecting antiques and library material. As far as we know, he made far fewer acquisitions of true art.

The hypothesis that Lorenzo commissioned Botticelli's *Allegory of Spring*, the most famous and popular painting of the period, as a gift for his cousin Lorenzo di Pierfrancesco on the occasion of his marriage to Semiramide Appiani in 1482 remains unproven. It is also debatable whether the painting was in fact commissioned by his brother Giuliano, between 1477 and 1478, to celebrate the imminent birth of his son Giulio.

It is quite certain that both it and the so-called *Pallas and the Centaur* (or, as I would prefer it, *Humility defeating Arrogance*) now in the Uffizi were in the "old home" of Pierfrancesco's family in the Via Larga at the end of the century, with other works by Botticelli, which proves that Lorenzo's cousins were particularly fond of the artist.

Lorenzo also had occasion to use Botticelli several times, and he included him in his plans to modernize the Spedaletto, the ancient Monastero degli Ospedalieri d'Altopascio near Volterra. Cronaca was architecturally responsible for the building's conversion to a villa during the early 1490s and the loggia was decorated by some of Central Italy's greatest painters, including Botticelli, Ghirlandaio, Perugino and Filippino Lippi.

A precedent had been set for this sort of collaborative effort when the walls of the Sistine Chapel at the Vatican were frescoed in 1481-82. The loss of the frescoes at the Spedaletto (the remains of which, damaged by the onslaughts of damp and fire, were looked for during in-depth research for Lorenzo's celebratory year) means that there is now no physical evidence of one of Lorenzo's final,

now mature commissions. An indirect reflection of the "Spedaletto style", which one imagines as elegant and precisely executed, can be found in the two monumental centred painted panels that Vasari claims Lorenzo "had made" for the Abbey of San Giusto near Volterra, of which his son Giuliano had the title. One of these is Ghirlandaio's *Christ in Glory*, featuring local devotional Saints and the abbot, now in the Pinacoteca in Volterra, the other the *Coronation of the Virgin with Saints* by Ghirlandaio and Botticelli and their assistants, now in the Bass Museum in Miami.

As works went on at the Spedaletto, the relationship of trust between Lorenzo and Filippino Lippi (son of Filippo) grew steadily stronger. He was the only one of the four artists not to have worked on the Sistine Chapel and had worked with his father on the frescoes in the Duomo at Spoleto. After his father's death he studied art under Botticelli, who had been his own father's pupil and assistant as well as Verrocchio's. In this exhibition an exquisite small painting of the *Madonna del Mare* testifies to the integration of the two masters from the same workshop (a question that needs to be addressed and clarified). The painting came from the Convento di Santa Felicita and is now in the Accademia. Its attribution has oscillated between Botticelli and his circle and the young Filippino, but is now almost certainly thought to be by the latter. The gentler design and softer working would appear to be the hand of Filippino, as would the misty marine landscape punctuated with pale azure mountains, reminiscent of Leonardo.

Of all the great Florentine *ateliers* of the Laurentian period, the one most difficult to do justice to in an exhibition is that of the Ghirlandaio family, headed by Domenico and including David and Benedetto as well as their relative by marriage Sebastiano Mainardi. Ghirlandaio was a great "master of walls", a master of the art of the fresco, taking on important commissions with a clutch of major and minor artists as assistants and often also bringing in independent artists in a sort of temporary collaboration, known as a "compagnia".

Bartolommeo di Giovanni, who had a workshop of his own, was one of these. He is known to have worked for Ghirlandaio, painting the parts of secondary importance – in fact he was conventionally known as *Alunno di Domenico* or "Pupil of Domenico" until he was formally identified by means of documentary evidence. The predella of Ghirlandaio's altarpiece of the *Adoration of the Magi* from the Spedale degl'Innocenti (1485-88) has been chosen to represent his work. Ghirlandaio gave Bartolommeo a contract to paint the predella, which is all his own work, having used him as his assistant for the *Slaughter of the Innocents* in the altarpiece. The seven stories are reproduced in his own graceful and concise style, developed as a result of his having painted small works for back rests and coffers, and feature his inimitable atonic, grim faces. Bartolommeo is known to have assisted Botticelli occasionally, as part of a system of exchange between the various workshops. Another instance of this is Biagio d'Antonio, who worked for two powerful art organisations – Ghirlandaio's workshop and the one headed by Cosimo Rosselli.

There is a great deal more to be said about the truly representative masters such as Cosimo Rosselli, who trained Piero di Cosimo, Andrea Feltrini, Fra Bartolomeo and Mariotto Albertinelli. There are the Pollaiolo brothers, Antonio and Piero; and the former's *Archangel Michael*, circa 1460-70, from the Museo Bardini is in the exhibition.

Returning to the subject of Lorenzo de' Medici in his role as a commissioner of works of figurative art, there appear to have been relatively few artistic purchases for private use (whereas the Library and Treasure House were vastly enlarged). However his clearness of intent and discernment of taste were denoted on a public level by the very exacting *programmes* he launched, although these were not necessarily always followed through. His view that artistic output should be channelled outwards was propagandist to a certain extent, and this is confirmed by his policy of sending artists to various other courts and by several instances of direct and indirect commissions for political and ethical purposes throughout the Florentine state.

It was undoubtedly the desire to pay homage to the glories of the state in a religious *pantheon* that led Lorenzo to place Benedetto da Maiano's marble bust of Giotto (1490) in the Cathedral of Santa Maria del Fiore, inside an antique clypeus with an epigraph to match Brunelleschi's existing one. This decision had a precedent as far as Lorenzo was concerned in the commissioning of the memorial to Filippo Lippi in the Duomo in Spoleto (1488), which was possibly made by the sculptor Ambrogio Barocci from an elaborate and elegant design by Lippi's son Filippino. As well as being an exaltation of the glories of Florence, with their roots in the magnificence of their antique Roman past, the bust was a vehicle for Lorenzo's great interest in mosaic which, apart from being a brilliant technique in terms of material, satisfied his passion for refined and ornamental pieces. In addition to collecting Byzantine mosaic-work, Lorenzo commissioned large and small mosaics (he kept some of the latter in his own room), and wanted to line the intrados of the cupola of Santa Maria del Fiore, which Brunelleschi had left devoid of ornamentation, with stuccoes and mosaics, in continuity with and emulating the domed vault of the nearby Baptistry. It is not mere chance, therefore, that Giotto's portrait in the Duomo shows him working at a mosaic. The mosaic exhibited here (an exceptional loan from the Opera del Duomo di Firenze) illustrates the final stage of an ambitious project launched under the auspices of Lorenzo il Magnifico: the mosaic decoration of the crypt under the high altar in the Duomo where the sacred remains of St Zenobius, Bishop were entombed. Work started on the decoration in 1491 and involved Botticelli, the Ghirlandaio family, Gherardo di Giovanni and his brother Monte, who were well-known illuminators. Works broke off when the Medicis were expelled from Florence in 1494 and were due to restart in 1504 when the Opera del Duomo announced a competition between David Ghirlandaio and Monte, the winner – who proved to be Monte – being commissioned to take charge of the decoration. His entry was, in fact, this magnificent mosaic which was a masterful alternation of tiny glazed cubes (or *tesserae*) and precious stones, now restored to its original power and splendour. Like many of Lorenzo's projects, however, the decoration of the crypt was eventually abandoned and never completed.

As we said initially, there was a strong ethical motive behind the conception and execution of the glazed terracotta frieze on the villa at Poggio a Caiano which, although situated in a private home, served as a delightful public statement or "manifesto" because of its location on the pediment of the villa, visible from outside.

The photograph of the Poggio frieze brings us to the high quality of the few sculptural works in this section, chosen chiefly to illustrate the dialogue between painting and sculpture in the areas of maximum contiguity but bearing in mind the obvious difficulties of transportation. Practical problems dissuaded us from our initial plan, which was to exhibit painted stucco reliefs, which are particularly appropriate to the theme of integration between the various artistic workshops. As has already been said, visitors to the exhibition would be well advised to round off this section with a visit to the Victoria & Albert Museum to see their fine collection of Florentine works.

This essay would be incomplete without even a very brief reference to the enormous activity of the Della Robbia workshop, favoured by the Medici family from the time of their introduction to Luca Della Robbia, founder of the family firm. The statues and reliefs executed in glazed terracotta, using the technique known autonomously as "Robbianesque" are all painted in the glorious bright fast colours that are their hallmark: blue and white initially, followed by yellow, green and purple in order to achieve the most captivating naturalism. Andrea, Luca's nephew, made the haughty Pesaro *Joshua*, an antique *imago clipeata* thought to be from the late 1460s. The two religious works come from the late Laurentian era: the *Cristo in Pietà* from the Monte di Pietà or Presto di San Martino with its fragile sorrowful beauty and the *St Sebastian* from Montalcino, whose Hellenistic appearance, grandiose in spite of their size, promotes the heroic concept of the martyr, which Savonarola's vehement spirituality had exalted and upheld.

Selected Bibliography

M. Wackernagel: *Der Lebensraum des Künstlers in der florentinischen Renaissance: Aufgaben und Auftraggeber, Werkstatt und Kunstmarkt*, Leipzig 1938.

A. Chastel: *Art et Humanisme a Florence au temps de Laurent le Magnifique*, Paris 1959.

E. H. Gombrich: *The Early Medici as Patrons of Art, in Italian Renaissance Studies: A Tribute to the late Cecilila M. Ady*, 1960 (in *Norm and Form. Studies in the Art of the Renaissance,* London and New York 1966).

M. Baxandall: *Painting and Experience in Fifteenth Century Italy*, Oxford 1972.

B. Cole: *The Renaissance Artist at Work*, New York 1983.

La pittura in Italia. Il Quattrocento, vol. 2, Milan 1987.

R. Lightbown: *Sandro Botticelli. Life and Work*, New York 1989.

F. Borsi (ed.): '*Per bellezza, Per studio, Per piacere'. Lorenzo il Magnifico e gli spazi dell'arte*, Florence 1991.

M. Gregori, A. Paolucci, C. Acidini Luchinat (ed.), *Maestri e botteghe. Pittura a Firenze alla fine del Quattrocento* (Florence), Milan 1992.

Eredità del Magnifico, Exhibition catalogue, Florence 1992.

Tabernacle-Shaped Frame,
late 15th century
Gilt on wood; 100 x 132 cm, inner
dimensions 69.5 x 82 cm
Florence, Palazzo Davanzati,
Museo della Casa Fiorentina

Bernardo di Stefano Rosselli
Descent of the Holy Spirit
Altar-frontal, 15th century;
Tempera on panel; 98 x 241 cm
Florence, Church of Santo Spirito

Master of the Johnson Nativity
Virgin of Mercy
Wood panel, 123 x 102 cm
Florence, Church of Santo Spirito,
Velluti Chapel

Pseudo Pier Francesco Fiorentino
**Adoration of the Christ Child with
Young Saint John**
Wood panel; 110 x 68 cm
Florence, Museo Bardini

Neri di Bicci
**"Christus Triumphans" between
God and Saints Benedict, Apollonia
and Francis; "Christus Patiens"
between God, the Virgin, Saint John
the Evangelist and Saint Mary
Magdalene**
Panel; 57 x 48.5 cm
Fiesole, Museo Bandini

Bartolomeo di Giovanni
Annunciation, Baptism of Christ, Marriage of the Virgin, Descent from the Cross, Presentation at the Temple, Martyrdom of Saint John the Evangelist, Saint Antonino Consecrates the Church of the

Innocents
Wood panels; 23 x 58 cm, 23 x 53 cm, 23 x 53 cm, 23 x 52 cm, 23 x 51 cm, 23 x 54 cm, 23 x 59 cm
Florence, Museo dello Spedale degli Innocenti

Sandro Botticelli
Madonna and Child with Saint John
15th century
Tempera on canvas; 134 x 92 cm
Florence, Galleria Palatina
(Inv. no. 357)

Filippo Lippi (attr.)
Madonna of the Sea
15th century
Oil on wood panel; 40 x 28 cm
Florence, Galleria dell'Accademia
(Inv. 1890 no. 8456)

Francesco Botticini (attr.)
Angels Playing Musical Instruments
last quarter 15th century
Tempera on panel; 36 x 121 cm
Empoli, Museo della Collegiata
di Sant'Andrea (Inv. no. 28)

Jacopo del Sellaio
Annunciation
1473
137 x 37 cm (2)
Florence, Church of Santa Lucia
dei Magnoli

Francesco Botticini
**Archangel Raphael and Tobiolo,
with Young Man in Prayer**
Wood panel; 156 x 89 cm
Florence, Sacristy Santa Maria del
Fiore (on loan from the Gallerie
Fiorentine)

Master of Marradi
**Nebuchadnezzar questions Daniel
and His Companions**
15th century
Tempera on wooden panel
Collection of Alberto Bruschi,
Grassina (Florence)

Monte di Giovanni
Head of Saint Zanobi
Mosaic; 91 x 60 cm
Florence, Museo dell'Opera
del Duomo

Andrea della Robbia
Christ
15th century
Enamelled terracotta; 70 x 105 cm
Florence, Collection Cassa
di Risparmio di Firenze

Andrea della Robbia
Joshua
1465-1470
Enamelled terracotta;
42.2 cm diameter
Pesaro, Museo dell'Ateneo Pesarese

Andrea della Robbia
Saint Sebastian
15th century
Enamelled terracotta; 126 cm h.
Montalcino, Museo Civico e d'Arte
Sacra

Lorenzo Patron and Collector

The Garden of San Marco
Direction of the Casa Buonarroti

Today there is still a garden overlooking the Piazza San Marco which is documented as having belonged to the Medici family during the second half of the 15th century, almost certainly from the 1470s. By 1480 the site was famous enough to be included in itineraries for illustrious visitors to Florence, and the garden plan featured on maps of the city. Indeed the characteristic row of cypress trees can still be seen if you look towards the Piazza San Marco from the Via Cavour.

Lorenzo set up a School there for would-be artists of his choice, and there were several buildings in the garden that were used for studying, eating and sleeping. The youngsters worked beneath the arches of the portico, alongside Bertoldo di Giovanni, the famous sculptor who had studied under Donatello and who was a friend of the Medici family. The young artists used the remains of unwanted sculptures lying under the loggia among the plants and tubs as materials – more important and complete sculptures were displayed in the Palazzo Medici. It is possible, but not definite, that there may also have been works by famous contemporary artists in the workshop – not finished paintings or sculptures, but drawings, cartoons or models.

The garden of San Marco was ransacked in November 1494 when Piero de' Medici, Lorenzo's son, was banished from Florence, and in November 1495 it was acquired by Giovanni Bentivoglio, *Signore* of Bologna and a friend of the Medici family.

Giorgio Vasari records Francesco Granacci, Giuliano Bugiardini, Lorenzo di Credi and Niccolò Soggi as having been among the artists who studied in the garden; and Pietro Torrigiano, Giovan Francesco Rustici, Baccio da Montelupo and Andrea Sansovino were among the sculptors. The young Leonardo da Vinci was probably one of the School's first pupils, in about 1475. Fifteen years later it was the adolescent Michelangelo's turn, which Vasari also records, and indeed he was described in a letter of 1494 as an "*ischultore dal giardino*". In fact the *Battle of Lapiths and Centaurs*, a brilliant interpretation of a mythological theme suggested by Poliziano, was begun here. This masterpiece by the very young Michelangelo was undoubtedly the finest work to have been produced by the 'nursery' garden of San Marco and it is an example of the workshop's gradual change of style towards the Mannerism of the 16th century.

During the course of the 15th century the Florentines began to be interested in the art of the past, and a few collections of antiques were started. The most important collection belonged to the Medici family, and this included gems, coins, marble and bronze statues, ceramics etc., most of which came from Rome. Most of Lorenzo de' Medici's antiques were displayed in the salons, courtyard and garden of the palace in Via Larga (now Via Cavour) and in the garden overlooking the Piazza San Marco.

From the second half of the 15th century the workshops of Verrocchio and the Pollaiolo brothers had the monopoly over Florence's artistic output. They produced works in gold, paintings and sculpture and sophisticated anatomical drawings of the nervous system. There still exist numerous copies of Antonio Pollaiolo's *Battle of the Nudes* and of the bronze statue of a satyr which was based on an antique work, yet unidentified, which were typical of the new figurative ideals.

The fine idealism that inspired the early 15th century Florentine artists (Brunelleschi, Donatello, Masaccio) soon became outmoded, and Lorenzo's followers developed a taste for "the antique" – elegant, sumptuous and subtle. Public commissions declined and most of the advances in the art world were confined to works destined for private collections. In the field of interior decoration, antique themes were favoured for painted and carved furnishings in most of the great houses in Florence, including the Palazzo Medici. Bertoldo's finely chiselled bronzes were very popular and Vasari describes him as being the curator of the Medici collections of sculpture, and he trained the young artists in the School at San Marco. Francesco Granacci, then twenty years old, introduced Michelangelo Buonarroti to the garden of San Marco in 1490. Michelangelo was six years younger than him, and they were both originally apprenticed to Ghirlandaio. These, then, are some of the background facts and notions of taste to be borne in mind when studying Michelangelo's *Battle of the Lapiths and Centaurs*, which he started carving in 1492 but never finished.

Lorenzo de' Medici set great store by the glories of the Florentine figurative tradition: it was he who commissioned the monuments to Filippo Lippi in Spoleto Cathedral and to Giotto in Florence Cathedral.

Michelangelo's vocabulary was strictly personal and polemic, acquired from many of the city's artists (Giotto, Masaccio and Donatello, to name but a few), it was certainly neither adulatory nor erudite. Michelangelo's *Madonna of the Stairs* was in strict contrast to the sophisticated, decadent and super-elegant world of the Medicis. It was both a return to Donatello's technique for flat *rilievo schiacciato*, and a departure. Donatello was regarded as having been one of the most versatile sculptors of all time, and the palace was full of his work. Though he had died twenty years before Michelangelo started working, the *Madonna of the Stairs* was a direct challenge to several of Donatello's works.

Michelangelo continually pressed Bertoldo for stories about Donatello, of which he could never have enough. Bertoldo himself had studied under Donatello and his own brilliant style had taken a – literally – archaeological turn. Thus Michelangelo was responsible for relaunching Donatello, though with no retrospective or conservatorial intent, and the latter's early 15th century work continued to fascinate many young artists. One of his most famous and respected works was the relief of the *Madonna and Child*, which was in Piero del Pugliese's collection at the end of the 15th century inside a tabernacle painted by the young Bartolomeo della Porta. The style of this young artist, later to become Fra Bartolomeo, was sober, individual and out of keeping with the current fashion, rather like the young Michelangelo's, though in a different field. It did not take long for Michelangelo's new ideas to take hold among some of his peers, who took their lead from him in painting and sculpture. However, by the end of the Quattrocento, in spite of Lorenzo il Magnifico's cunning political propaganda, Florence no longer held supremacy in the artistic field: the "maniera moderna" or Mannerism originated in fact in Milan, between the ages of Bramante and Bramantino, with Leonardo's *Last Supper*, and the future of Italian art was to appear under Roman skies.

Artists and writers frequently moved in the rarified circles of 15th century courtly life, particularly those that revolved around Lorenzo de' Medici. The artists offered advice and opinions on the antique works and painted important men for posterity, as well as infants and the beauties of the moment. Portraits thus became a sought-after art form, highly prized as possessions and presents. Writers provided titles, works and epigraphs for sculptures and paintings and sometimes made up poems or prose in honour of particularly distinguished antique or modern works.

The relationship between art and humanism in Florence was not unconnected with the personal tastes, sympathies and idiosyncrasies of the *literati*. It was often the relationship traced between certain artists and the *literati*, as they went from court to court, that determined the fate of the regional art schools in Renaissance Italy.

Artists and *literati* all moved in the same circles, where everybody knew everybody else and they all conformed to the latest trend. They were sentimental and certainly liked to think of themselves as "old-school".

With the betrayal in November 1494 of Lorenzo's son Piero de' Medici, the *ambience* created around the garden at San Marco began to crumble. In September of the same year Angelo Poliziano, the author who had suggested the theme of the *Battle of the Lapiths and Centaurs*, died in a house overlooking the garden.

In the meantime, some of the young artists who might have frequented the School had left Florence: Leonardo had been in Milan for several years, Andrea Sansovino had gone off to find fortune in Portugal, and Pietro Torrigiano had set out for Bologna and then Rome, after punching Michelangelo on the nose during a fight and disfiguring him for life. Soon Baccio da Montelupo was to leave for Bologna and then Venice.

Michelangelo had already left in October 1494, and gone to stay in Bologna with Giovanfrancesco Aldovrandi for a year, to study Dante, Petrarch and Boccaccio.

During the celebrations in honour of the fifth centenary of Lorenzo il Magnifico's death, the Casa Buonarroti, where the *Madonna of the Stairs* and the *Battle of the Lapiths and Centaurs* are housed, organized an exhibition entitled "Il Giardino di San Marco – Maestri e compagni del giovane Michelangelo". The exhibition contained pivotal works by artists from earlier generations, from Donatello to Mantegna, alongside works by some of the young artists mentioned above. Works were borrowed from museums and institutions both in Italy and abroad, and our intention was to recall an experience which, although short-lived, was to have far-reaching and long-lasting effects.

Text taken from P. Barocchi (ed.), *Il Giardino di San Marco*, Exhibition catalogue (Florence), Milan 1992 (with bibliography). Courtesy of the Direction of the Casa Buonarroti.

The Medici Collection of Antique Treasures House
Direction of the Museo degli Argenti

The wealth of the Medici family, initially accumulated by Averardo, known as Bicci (1360-1428) and then augmented by his sons Cosimo (1389-1464) and Lorenzo (1395-1440), both bankers and men of influence, endowed them with a consistent source of economic power which allowed them (Cosimo in particular, who had a strong network of intermediaries at his beck and call) to acquire very precious antiques and curios of all sorts. Although the famous cornelian of Apollo and Marsyas, now in the Museo Archeologico in Naples, belonged to Cosimo, as Ghiberti recounts in his *Commentari*, it was with Piero di Cosimo (1416-1469), known as "Piero the Gouty" that the family collections began to gain momentum. The "Scrittoio" in the palace in the Via Larga, buit by Michelozzo, housed the antique and modern vases with their precious mounts, the cameos, the incised precious stones and medals, coins and plaques of which there were more than two thousand altogether according to the inventory of the possessions of Lorenzo il Magnifico (1449-1492) at the time of his death. The whole family was seized with such a passion for collecting that its collections even contained unicorn horns, elephant tusks and instruments made from exotic animal trophies. However the antique statues and precious *objets d'art* formed the nucleus of the collection.

The statues were the subject of recent research by Laurie Fusco and Gino Corti, as part of the Laurentian celebrations. Most of these stood originally in the garden next to the palace, conceived as a medieval *hortus conclusus* and hidden from the world by high walls which jealously guarded the treasures.

It has been demonstrated that the statues were set out according to a didactic and metaphoric plan. Thus two statues of Marsyas, one flayed and the other seated, were positioned at the entrance to the garden, facing each other, as an example of the destiny awaiting those who displease Apollo, god of the arts and lord of the garden. Despite his lofty connections, Lorenzo failed to acquire the so-called "Belvedere" Apollo – later named after its location – which Della Rovere bought for himself in 1489 having received news of the celebrated findings at the convent of San Lorenzo Panisperna in Rome. Thanks to the good offices of the antiquarian Giovanni Ciampolini, Lorenzo did manage to obtain a fine group of three satyrs which has been recognized as being either the work in Graz or that still in the Florentine collections.

"The Magnificent" also owned an Eros "shooting his bow", now fragmented but preserved in the Museo Archeologico in Florence, which is apparently a replica of the same type as the one from which Jacopo Alari Bonacolsi, known as "l'Antico" worked his famous

bronze. Lorenzo was just as fond of busts and antique heads, and many of these were found in the cupboards and recesses of the palace when the inventory was made after his death. Recent research has shed more light on several of these sculptures, amongst which was a bust of the Emperor Nerva, larger than life but still untraced. The Medici interest in iconography, which Filarete mentioned after his visits to the palace in Florence, was already a determining factor in Piero's (Lorenzo's father) collecting, and according to Filarete: "... he has the effigies and the images of all the Emperors and men of honour, some in gold, some in silver, some in bronze, some in semi-precious stones, some in marble and other materials that are marvellous to behold [...] so that he, taking pleasure in one or other of them, declaims at length the dignity of the image [...] captured so beautifully by its maker".

In 1471, Lorenzo was sent as ambassador to Rome on the occasion of the coronation of the Pope and received, as he notes in his Ricordi, two marble busts: one of Agrippa and one of Augustus which, later restored, are in all probability identifiable as the two busts now in the Uffizi. There is also a bust of Hadrian in the Uffizi that can be traced through the inventory as having been placed in the passage-way between the courtyard and the ancestral Medici palace. Together with a "sleeping Cupid", also now in the Uffizi, and a "female nude more lifelike than the real thing", it can be identified as one of the antiques that Vasari recalls as having been a gift from Ferdinand I of Aragon brought to Florence by Giuliano da Sangallo. The *antiquarium* situated in the garden loggia contained several reliefs, amongst others a putto holding Jove's thunderbolt, part of a group of similar well-known pieces which were thought throughout the Renaissance to be the work of either Praxiteles or Polycletus. Due also to Vasari's records, other reliefs have been identified, as "Adonis with a very fine dog", an another relief of a meeting between two heroes and a rare representation of Kairos. The latter, based on a famous statue by Lysippus, personified the idea of Opportunity, of the Eternal and the Fleeting Moment, and must have been particularly dear to Lorenzo given its iconographical relevance to his own philosophical interests.

Lorenzo's passionate adherence to Platonism, which Ficino had equated with Christian morality, led to a lengthy search for a bust of the philosopher, which Girolamo Rossi da Pistoia finally managed to track down in Greece, and finally bought in Athens. There is a Greek marble sculpture in the Uffizi thought to be the statue discovered near the Platonic Academy, but the features, despite the inscription on the base, are not Plato's as we know them from a herm now in Berlin. This, together with the fact that the precise location of the Academy was not then known, leads one to conclude that a certain amount of deception may well have gone into satisfying the repeated demands of the illustrious Florentine.

This hypothesis comes as no great surprise, there are documents confirming that fake gems were offered to Lorenzo, as were mediocre works at astronomic prices which he, well-advised as always, seems mostly to have avoided.

The importance of this collection for contemporary artists was enormous, since it provided them with classical models to study in order to emulate their beauty. Great masters like Verrocchio, who is thought to have worked on the seated Marsyas previously mentioned, restored the statues to perfect condition. This was also the case with the "Red Marsyas", which can be seen in all its glory at the beginning of the second corridor in the Uffizi, which may well have been converted into the figure of Christ before Cosimo acquired it, judging by the fact that the bust had been broken off at the shoulders so that the arms subsequently required complete restoration. Lorenzo's passion for antiques can be traced through a great many of his gems which have ended up in the Museo Archeologico in Naples, through the Farnese family, and then transferred to Naples. It is easy to imagine, though, what sort of an effect his treasures must have had on his contemporaries. There were some absolutely unique pieces, like the famous *Farnese Cup*, which had an apotheosis scene on the *recto* containing precise Nilotic allusions and the most beautiful "gorgoneion" imaginable on the *verso*. This "...bowl of sardonyx and chalcedony and agate, with figures on the inside and a head of Medusa on the outside, weight 2 pounds 6 ounces" was valued at the astronomic figure of ten thousand florins at the time of Lorenzo's death. A great deal has been written about this and other carved pieces, on which Lorenzo often had the letters LAV.R.MED. inscribed to denote his ownership. If the chalcedony with the centaur holding up a basket was the model for one of the tondi in the courtyard of the Medici Palace in the Via Larga, which was one of Michelozzo's workshop's greatest achievements, then the other figurations decorating the courtyard may also have close links with the Laurentian cornelians and agates. This continuous connection between antique and modern works and eclectic and erudite curios also extended to the collection of precious vases in the "scrittoio degli anelli". Many of them are still instantly recognizable because of the inscription they bear, which is identical to the one on the gems.

The vases remained untouched during the events leading up to the partial sack of the Palazzo Medici (1494) and, together with other jewels confiscated by the Republicans, were subsequently bought back by Lorenzo di Giovanni Tornabuoni once he was safely in Rome (from 1495).

Others still were considered as part of the dowry of Alfonsina Orsini, wife of Piero di Lorenzo de' Medici (1472-1503), whilst even the Nerli family managed to acquire some pieces, including at least four vases from Lorenzo's collection and the famous *Naked with Fear* and a *Bronze Hercules Blocking the Path of a Lion*, which were still in their possession in 1502. It is likely that the collections were reformed on Alessandro de' Medici's return to Florence since, on his death, Margaret of Austria took all her husband's treasures away with her as a guarantee of her dowry, which came in useful at the time of her second marriage to Ottavio Farnese. Although the Medici family would never accept the fact, they were unable to recuperate the famous Farnese Cup or the so-called "Seal of Nero". Cardinal Giovanni de' Medici, when Leo X, used the vases in his posession as relic containers and some were returned to Florence, possibly as early as 1515-1516, during the course of his visit to the city.

It was only with Clement VII, however, that they were definitely bought to the city. It was he who commissioned the Tribunal of the Relics ("delle reliquie") designed by Michelangelo for the church of San Lorenzo, where most of the Laurentian vases were placed (1532), apart from the few that were still in the Pope's treasure house at Castel Sant'Angelo in 1572.

They remained in their religious surroundings for some two hundred years, shown to the faithful only at Easter, until they attracted the historical and naturalistic curiosity of Giuseppe Bencivenni Pelli in 1778. In 1785 he managed to obtain some of them in exchange for one hundred reliquaries donated by the Grand Duke of Lorraine together with a new chapel to house the relics. The vases made of rock crystal remained at San Lorenzo, as they were considered quite suitable for the display of sacred remains, the vases made of semi-precious stones were mostly removed from their mounts; some were sent to the Florentine naturalistic collections and are now to be found in the Museo di Mineralogia in the University of Florence.

Most of them were displayed, untouched, in the Uffizi (which had been "reordered" in 1782) and eventually came to their present location, the Museo degli Argenti. As a whole, they represent the most impressive group of objects of their kind from the 15th century, each of them revealing different aspects of the character and interests of the patron who collected them, originating them from France, Burgundy, Venice and the Levant. They were mounted by the best of Lorenzo's goldsmiths, amongst whom were the well-known Giusto da Firenze and possibly also Verrocchio himself, as Dora Liscia-Bemporad recently suggested during a conference. Crowned by the impresa of the diamond ring, which inscribes a silver globe with the red Medici bezants and the azure bezant bearing the fleur-de-lys, these precious containers still provoke amazement, while an illuminated inventory from the end of the 16th century illustrates the parts of the mountings that have been lost: a multitude of dragons and intertwined tendrils of laurel, known as "bronconi" or "knotty branches", also an allusion to

their noble owner. One of the many examples, a small lidded vase (Museo degli Argenti, Inv. 1921, no. 2442) in sardonyx, the vase itself late Roman, bears a rare variation of the Medici emblem: a diamond that appears to have erupted from the top of a mountain – yet another cryptic allusion to the Medicean virtues, although its mysterious symbolic vocabulary has yet to be deciphered. It is a message carried on through the ages, a sort of Sibylline humanist challenge to whoever is able to unravel yet another of these cultural conundrums.

Selected Bibliography

K. Ashengreen Piacenti: *Il Museo degli Argenti*, Milan 1967 (1968).

N. Dacos, N. Giuliano, U. Pannuti: *Il tesoro di Lorenzo il Magnifico, le gemme*, Florence 1973.

D. Heikamp, A. Grote: *Il tesoro di Lorenzo il Magnifico, i vasi,* Florence 1974.

L. Beschi: *Le antichità di Lorenzo il Magnifico; caratteri e vicende*, in *Gli Uffizi, quattro secoli di una galleria*, Conference Papers, Florence 1983, pp. 161-176.

L. Beschi: *I rilievi ravennati dei "troni"* in *Felix Ravenna*, CXXVIII-CXXX, 1984-1985, pp. 37-80.

H. Meyer: *Der weisse und der rote Marsyas*, Munich 1987.

M.L. Morricone Martini: *Giorgio Vasari e le "anticaglie": storia del "putto in pietra nera che dorme" alla Galleria degli Uffizi*, in *Atti Acc. Lincei Rend. Morali*, XLIV, 1989, pp. 250-277.

A. Guidotti: *Gli arredi del palazzo nel tempo*, in *Palazzo Medici Riccardi di Firenze*, Florence 1990, pp. 244-256.

C. Acidini Luchinat: La *"Santa Antichità", la scuola, il Giardino e l'arte*, in '*Per bellezza, per studio, per piacere'. Lorenzo il Magnifico e gli spazi dell'arte*, F. Borsi (ed.), Florence 1991, pp. 99-161.

C. Acidini Luchinat: *Il Mecenate degli artisti*, in *Lorenzo il Magnifico*, Rome 1992, pp. 171-188.

K. Ashengreen Piacenti: *Itinerario laurenziano nel Museo degli Argenti*, Florence 1992.

E. Garberi Zorzi: *La collezione di Lorenzo nel Palazzo di via Larga*, in *Lorenzo il Magnifico*, Rome 1992, pp. 189-212.

Itinerario laurenziano, in *Gli Uffizi, studi e ricerche*, 10, 1992.

Libro d'inventario dei beni di Lorenzo il Magnifico, M. Spallanzani and G. Gaeta Bertelà (ed.), Florence 1992.

The Library
Cristina Acidini Luchinat, together with the Direction of the
Biblioteca Medicea Laurenziana

Lorenzo's enormous contribution to the expansion of the family library, started by his grandfather Cosimo and extended by his father Piero and his uncle Giovanni, has become increasingly apparent over the last ten years and was the subject of an exhibition at the Biblioteca Medicea Laurenziana at San Lorenzo in 1992. The exhibition, entitled "All'ombra del lauro" (or In the Shade of the Laurel), was the culmination of years of research. Lorenzo's additions to the family library had been studied almost exclusively in specialist publications.

This aspect of his passion for collecting is comparable to his more famous and well-researched love of precious antiquities, which he collected for his own "treasure house" and they differed from his patronage of the so-called "most important arts", which tended to be rather transient.

The collection of codices, frequently richly illuminated, with which he supplemented the already substantial family library, was regarded as second to none by virtue of its breadth and quality, not only by his contemporaries, but also when compared with the libraries of other noble houses in Italy and in Europe, such as those of the Aragon and Montefeltro families and of Matthias Corvinus for example. It was also the last great collection of manuscripts, whose greatest period of progression and expansion coincided with the advent of the incunabula and the printed word.

Lorenzo continued to add liberally to his library from various sources right up to the time of his death. He was advised and sometimes instructed by Agnolo Poliziano and Giovanni Lascari, the humanists and men of letters closest to him, and was able to buy codices both from Italy (obtained from the libraries of Filelfo and Francesco Sassetti) and from the East, which enabled him to acquire Greek texts until he died. Lorenzo also had other ways of acquiring new manuscripts.

All "dedicated" works had automatic right of entry to the library – these were works either especially commissioned for Lorenzo or presented to him as gifts, not just by well-known authors within his immediate circle such as Marsilio Ficino, Agnolo Poliziano, Pico della Mirandola and Luigi Pulci, but also, as was demonstrated by the selection of works chosen for the exhibition at the Laurentian Library, by a wide range of lesser known authors, whose work was respectfully and hopefully placed in the "shade of the laurel" in an attempt to win approval, attention and, sometimes, protection and favour.

Among the latters was Aurelio Lippo Brandolini's codex *De laudibus Laurentii Medicis libellus* (Plut.36.36), which is exhibited here. Brandolini came from a disgraced noble Florentine family exiled in Naples between 1472 and 1478. He addressed a panegyric to Lorenzo, together with epigrams addressed to Lorenzo and his younger brother Giuliano, in an attempt to regain Lorenzo's favour, invoking him as the guardian of the "absent", or exiled. The library also acquired his political treaty *De comparatione reipublicae et regni* (1490), also dedicated to Lorenzo.

Needless to say, the codices dedicated to Lorenzo by the great humanist *literati* and philosophers are much more culturally significant.

The exhibition contains Marsilio Ficino's codex of the *Traduzioni neoplatoniche* (Plut.82.15) – an example of Ficino's vital and fundamental role as an interpreter of ancient Neoplatonist philosophy – acceded to the library shortly after 1489. Among the humanist works by other classic authors are the *Commentarii in M. Valerium Martialem* (Plut.55.33), written by Domizio Calderini, apostolic secretary, presented to Lorenzo by the author in the summer of 1473, during a brief sojourn in Florence that coincided with the arrival of Pietro Riario, the new Bishop of Florence.

With the death of Matthias Corvinus, King of Hungary, on 4th April 1490, a considerable quantity of codices became unexpectedly available. The King had been a passionate bibliophile and had ordered a vast quantity of manuscripts from the Florentine copyists which after his death remained in the workshops. Many of them then found their way onto the shelves of the Medici library.

However, the codices that most accurately reflect Lorenzo's plans for a great library, intended not only for family use but also for scholars and friends, are the ones commissioned as part of a deliberate integration of missing or poorly represented authors, a project entrusted in part by Lorenzo to his eldest son Piero under the guidance of Poliziano.

It has been correctly observed that a great many religious texts were ordered as part of this project, leading one to assume that there were insufficient numbers of these in the library when it was inherited. There are, nevertheless, many works on other diverse literary subjects; St Bernard's *Expositio super cantica* (Plut.16.4) was one of the religious works acquired, and as examples of his predilection for classical authors, the codices of Marsilio Ficino's translations of Plotinus' *Enneadi* (Plut.82.11) and Livy's *Historiae* (Plut.63.2) are exhibited here.

Lorenzo's lively interest in music (this was the subject of one of the symposia held in Florence in 1992) is represented by Manuele Briennio's Greek manuscript (Plut.28.11); and his great appreciation of religious tradition and Tuscan history is demonstrated by the *Liber miraculorum s. Johannis abbatis*, which describes the miracles of San Giovanni Gualberto, who founded the Order of Vallombrosa, and by the stories of the Blessed Spirits and hermits of the Abbey which Fra Girolamo da Raggiolo wrote in response to a request Lorenzo himself made one day as they conversed walking through the gardens of the Abbey at Vallombrosa (Plut.18.21).

The common factor to the hard core of codices commissioned by Lorenzo, to which the ones ordered by his sons Piero and Giovanni, later Pope Leo X, have been added for reasons of logic and continuity, is that they all contain a large number of symbolic images. The so-called *divise* or "devices", known as *imprese* during the 16th century, were an important, if occasionally ambiguous, factor in terms of recognition. Some of these were freely adopted by various members of the family, rather like the coat of arms with the six balls or bezants, whereas others belonged strictly and almost exclusively to individuals. The device of the three feathers, in green, red and white (but white is also depicted in silver and azure in illuminations), first appeared during Cosimo's time, often coupled with the other Medici device of the diamond ring in other Medici commissions and therefore also to be found in the codices. There are numerous other devices chosen by Lorenzo from the world of symbolic imagery, each with its own underlying symbolic meaning, some of which have been deciphered and others which remain obscure.

The illuminated borders and ornate embellishments of Laurentian manuscripts often contain the laurel bush, the humanist metaphor for Lorenzo seen as the *laurus*; the dried or "knotty" branch once more in flower signifying the continuous renewal of life throughout time, to which the often repeated mottoes SEMPER and *Le tems revient* allude.

The butterflies fluttering over the flame, an ancient symbol of the soul (or psyche) attracted by the light, the six beehives, a reference to that most ordered of communities, symbol for many centuries of a well-regulated monarchy (perhaps, also a hidden reference to the orphic concept of the swarming of souls, like bees, from the Creator's breast), the parrot among the ears of millet, representing the joys of eloquence.

In Piero's codices there are devices whose meaning is even more obscure, the sun and the rain together; the lute with the broken string; the "knotty branch" giving out flames; two wheels smoothing and polishing a hard jasper. Even before Giovanni's election to the papacy in 1512, he adopted the *impresa* of the yoke with the motto SVAVE, representing the sweetness of obedience to God, common to the religious orders, sometimes accompanied by the letter N. The letter R appears mysteriously among the devices (undoubtedly the same as in the inscription *LAV.R.MED.* on the antique vases in the "treasure house") sometimes intact, sometimes broken to denote mourning; Anna Lenzuni's hypothesis that it should be taken to mean the initial letter of the Horatian appellation *Rex paterque* given to Maecenas, the greatest patron of ancient times, is a convincing one.

The enormous growth of the library, which absorbed much of Lorenzo's energies and finances during his later years, provided work for a great many copyists and illuminators. A tendency towards order and systematic editing, although not obligatory, is evinced by the general use of humanist cursive script (known as the "old-style bastard") which conferred a graphic uniformity. Lorenzo's tendency towards pluralism in the commissioning of works of art seems not to have applied in the case of the illuminations, which appear predominantly to have been the product of two workshops, headed by Attavante and Boccardino. Attavante's pages were sumptuous and he produced an enormous volume of work for very high-ranking clients between 1470 and the early 1500s. Apart from the Medici, he supplied Florence Cathedral and other important ecclesiastical institutions with choir books, breviaries and humanist codices, as well as Federico da Montefeltro and Matthias Corvinus. Boccardino was trained in Francesco d'Antonio del Chierico's workshop, well known for its Medici patronage, and had initially worked for Gherardo di Giovanni. He too supplied illuminated codices to Matthias Corvinus and to Lorenzo and he continued to supply these to Lorenzo's son Piero and to Laudomia Medici after Lorenzo's death.

In accordance with his general predilection for articles of refinement and sumptuous materials (reflected in his support for the revival of the art of mosaic), Lorenzo seems to have preferred small decorations, richly gilded and exquisitely finished, the racemes set with jewelled "studs", fake jewels and coins, *tondi* featuring personal and family devices and crests. There are other works of art hidden between the covers of the works in the Laurentian Library, however.

There is, for example, a superlative decoration in the codex with the *Vita di Apollonio Tianeo* transcribed by Flavio Filostrato in the translation by Alamanno Rinuccini (Plut.67.21), illuminated by Francesco Rosselli, brother of Cosimo the painter and a painter in his own right: the painted frame imitates the geometric tracery of an enamelled and gem-set necklace.

Finally, the precious bindings of the books added to their value as exquisite *objets d'art* rather than as instruments of learning. The books were bound in silk or velvet with plated frames and silver medallions, sometimes enamelled, the covers hinting at the fabulous illuminations to be discovered inside. Almost all the bindings were lost when the library suffered the consequences of the Medici expulsion in 1494; among the very few surviving original works, Petrarch's *Trionfi* in the Bibliothèque Nationale de Paris, presented to Charles VIII (Ital.584) is worth mentioning, as is Lucrezia di Lorenzo's Book of Hours in the Bayerische Staatsbibliothek in Munich (CLM 23639).

Selected Bibliography

E.B. Fryde: *Humanism and Renaissance Historiography*, London 1983.

F. Ames-Lewis: *The Library and Ma-* *nuscripts of Piero di Cosimo de' Medici*, New York and London 1984.

A. Garzelli (ed.): *Miniatura fiorentina del Rinascimento 1440-1525. Un primo censimento*, 2 vols. Florence 1985 (Tuscan inventories and catalogues, 18-19).

A.D. de la Mare: *Cosimo and His Books*, in *Cosimo 'il Vecchio' de' Medici 1389-1464*, Oxford 1992, pp. 115-156.

A. Lenzuni (ed.): *All'ombra del lauro. Documenti librari della cultura in età laurenziana*, Exhibition Catalogue (Florence), Milan 1992.

Treasure and antiquities

Head of a Horse
from the Medici Collection
2nd century BC ?
Bronze; 67 x 80.5 cm
Florence, Museo Archeologico

Head of a Horse
copy from the antique, 15th century
Bronze; h. 16.2 cm
Florence, Museo Archeologico

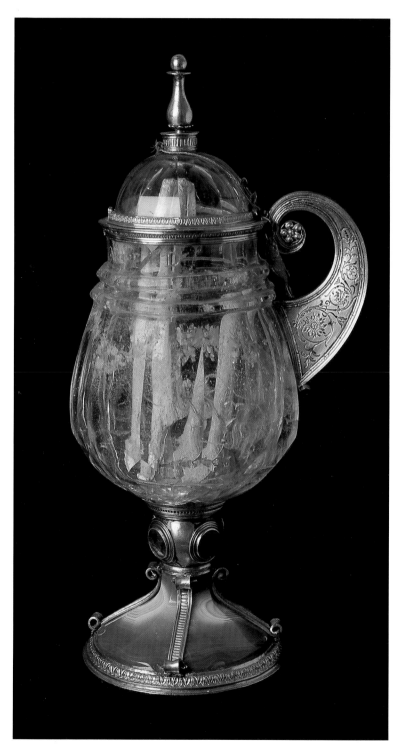

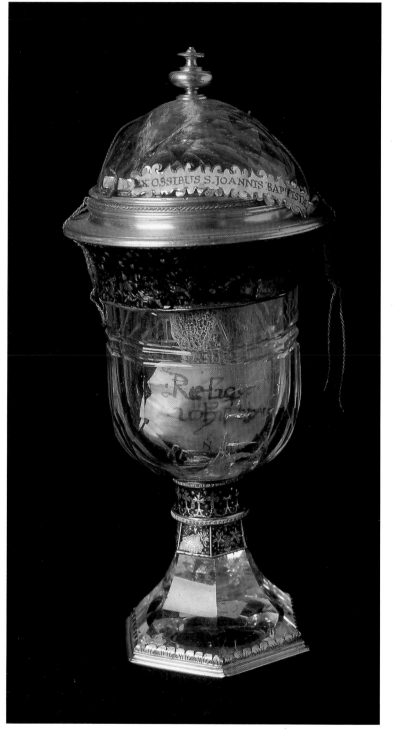

Vase with Lid
Rock crystal; the foot in purple and
grey agate with white veining;
30 cm h., 7.2 cm diameter;
diameter of the lid 6.5 cm; weight

1495 g; initialled LAV. R. MED.
Florence, San Lorenzo, Tesoro
(Inv.1945, no. 1)

Vase with Lid
Rock crystal; 21.2 cm h.; initialled
inside LAV. R. MED.
Florence, San Lorenzo, Tesoro
(Inv.1945, no. 116)

Cylindrical Vase with two Handles
Rock crystal; 32.4 cm h.
Florence, San Lorenzo, Tesoro
(Inv.1945, no. 87)

Vase with Lid
Sardonyx; the lid is the same quality
crystal as the vase; 10.2 cm h.,
diameter of lid 7 cm, weight 540 g;
initialled LAV. R. MED.
Florence, Museo degli Argenti
(Inv. 1945, no. 450)

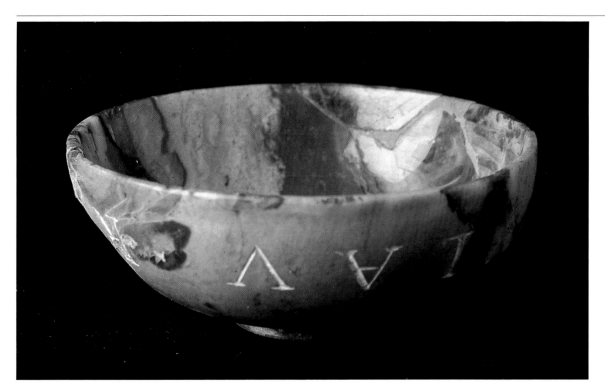

Double Cup
Red and pink diasper, cornelian, impure amethyst; highly polished; 4.2 cm h., diameter 11.5 cm; 0.4-0.5 cm thickness; initialled LAV. R. MED.
Florence, Museo di Mineralogia (Inv. 1947, no. 13210/206)

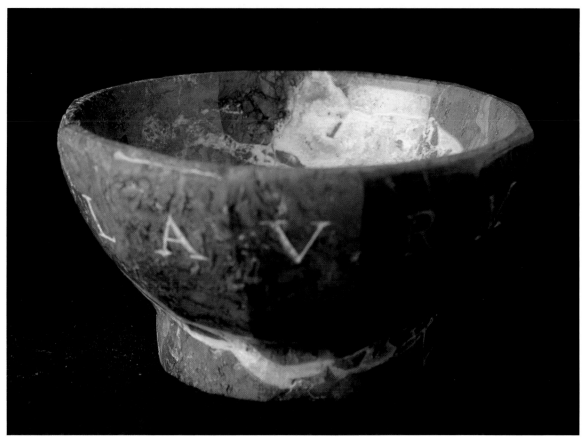

Cup
Red, brown and yellowish diasper with white veining, inferior quality; 5.5 cm h., diameter 10.7 cm; 0.5-0.9 cm thickness, weight 320 g; initialled LAV. R. MED.
Florence, Museo di Mineralogia (Inv. 1947, no. 13504/209)

The Garden of San Marco

Donatello and Fra Bartolomeo
Tabernacle of Piero del Pugliese
(open wings: *Nativity, Madonna and Child, Presentation in the Temple*)
Reconstructed photomontage

Donatello
Madonna and Child (Dudley Madonna)
c 1440
Marble; 27.2 x 16.5 cm
London, Victoria and Albert Museum (Inv. A 84-1927)

Fra Bartolomeo
Nativity/Archangel Gabriel Presentation
c 1497
Oil on wood panel; 20.2 x 8.9 cm
(on reverse 19.6 x 8.7 cm)
18.3 x 9.4 cm
(on reverse 17.8 x 9.2 cm)
Florence, Galleria degli Uffizi
(Inv. 1477)

Bertoldo di Giovanni
Hercules on Horseback
(undated)
Bronze; 30.5 cm h.
Modena, Galleria Estense
(Inv. 2265)

Michelangelo Buonarroti
Battle of Lapiths and Centaurs
1490-92
Marble; 80.5 x 88 cm (a cast of the
original is exhibited)
Florence, Casa Buonarroti
(Inv. 194)

Michelangelo Buonarroti
Madonna of the Stairs
c 1490
Marble; 56.7 x 40.1 cm
(a cast of the original is exhibited)
Florence, Casa Buonarroti
(Inv. 190)

Pietro Torrigiano
Saint Fina
c 1496
Painted marble; 58 cm h.; bears an
inscription: BEATAE FINAE VIRGINI
SACRUM
San Gimignano, Ospedale di Santa
Fina

Baccio da Montelupo
Head of Joseph of Arimathea
1494-95
Terracotta; 26 cm h.
Bologna, Museo di San Domenico

The Library

Aurelio Lippo Brandolini
De laudibus Laurentii Medicis libellus
Parchment; second half of 15th century; 185 x 130 mm; Neapolitan illumination; original Medicean binding
Florence, Biblioteca Medicea Laurenziana (Plut. 35.36)

Domizio Calderini
Commentarii in M. Valerium Martialem
Parchment; 1473; 270 x 190 mm; illumination attributed to Mariano del Buono; original Medicean binding
Florence, Biblioteca Medicea Laurenziana (Plut. 53.33)

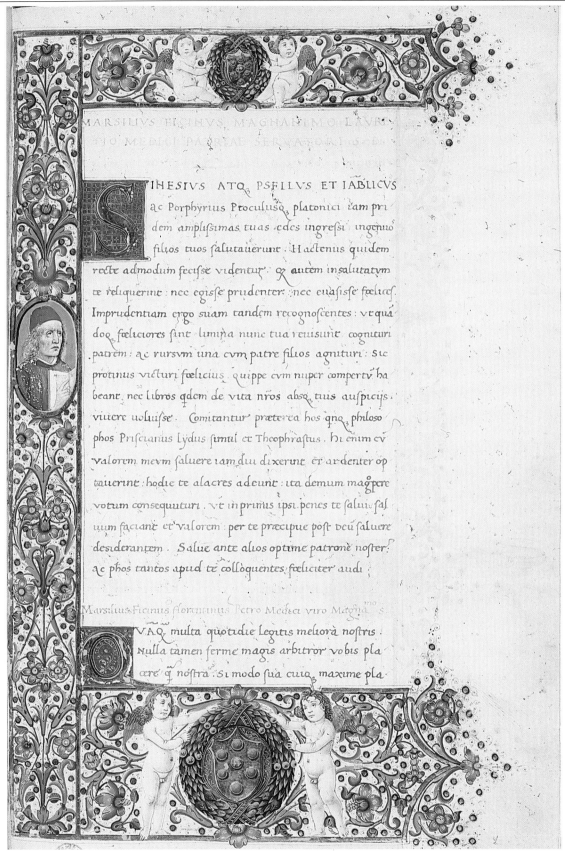

Marsilio Ficino
Neoplatonic Translation
Parchment; last quarter of 15th
century; 300 x 205 mm; original
Medicean binding
Florence, Biblioteca Medicea
Laurenziana (Plut. 82.15)

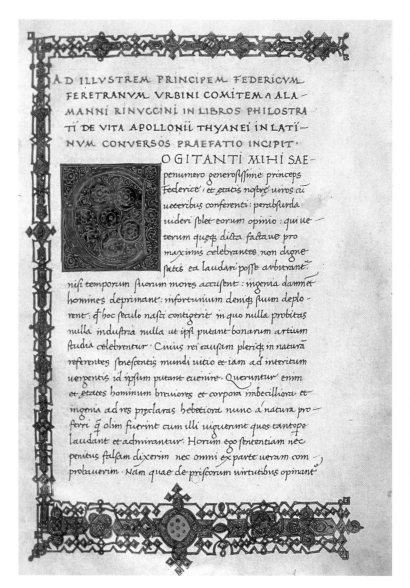

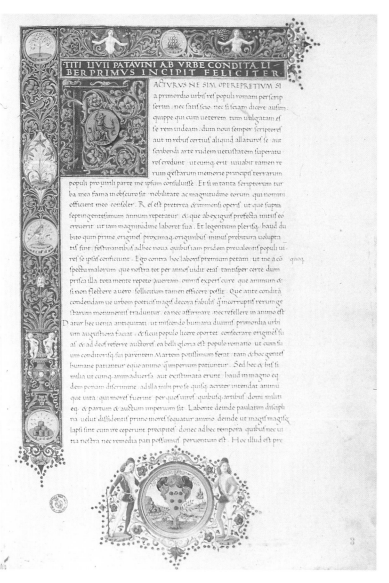

Flavio Filostrato
Life of Apollonio Tianeo, translated
by Alamanno Rinuccini
Parchment; 1475; 265 x 177 mm;
illuminated by Pietro Cennini;
original Medicean binding
Florence, Biblioteca Medicea
Laurenziana (Plut. 67.21)

Titus Livius
Ab urbe condita libri X
Parchment; 1466; 380 x 265 mm;
inscribed by Giovanni del Ciriago,
illuminated by Attavante; original
Medicean binding
Florence, Biblioteca Medicea
Laurenziana (Plut. 63.2)

Manuelis Bryenii, **De Musica,**
Michaelis Pselli, **Opuscula Quaedam**
Parchment; 15th century; 360 x 245
mm; illumination attributed to
Attavante; original Medicean binding
Florence, Biblioteca Medicea
Laurenziana (Plut. 28.11)

Plotino
Enneadi, translated and annotated
by Marsilio Ficino
Parchment; 1490 (except the letter
on reverse of page 40); 350 x 250
mm; inscribed by Luca Fabiani,
illuminated by Attavante; original
Medicean binding
Florence, Biblioteca Medicea
Laurenziana (Plut. 82.11)

Bartolomeo Fonzio
Explanatio in Persium Poetam
Parchment; 15th century; 218 x 143
mm; original Medicean binding
Florence, Biblioteca Medicea
Laurenziana (Plut. 54.23)

San Bernardo
Super Cantica Canticorum
Salomonis expositio
Parchment; 1491; 370 x 250 mm;
possibly inscribed by Neri di Filippo
Rinuccini; original Medicean binding
Florence, Biblioteca Medicea
Laurenziana (Plut. 16.4)

Girolamo da Raggiolo
Liber miraculorum s. Johannis
abbatis e **Chronicon beatorum**
patrum ordinis Vallisumbrosae
Parchment; 15th century; 260 x 184
mm; inscribed by ser Jacopo de'
Dinuzi di San Gimignano (?);
original Medicean binding, missing
chain and one clasp
Florence, Biblioteca Medicea
Laurenziana (Plut. 18.21)

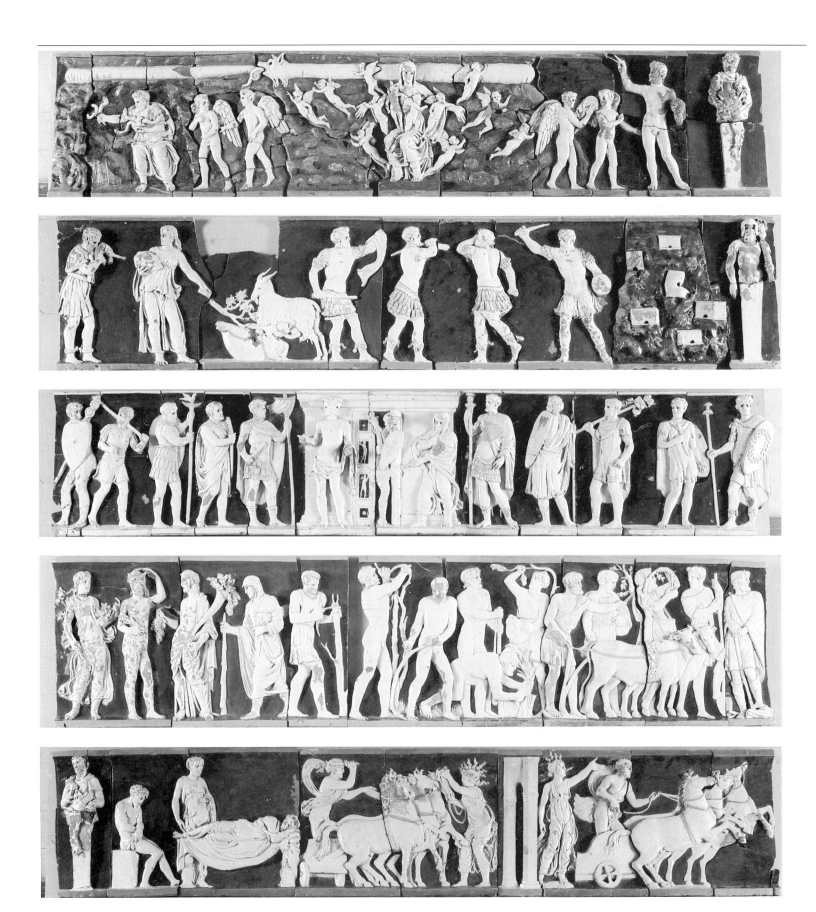

Enamelled terracotta frieze from the
Villa di Poggio a Caiano

In the Sign of Janus
Cristina Acidini Luchinat

The glazed terracotta frieze, roughly 18 metres long, which decorates the pediment of the facade of Lorenzo de' Medici's villa at Poggio a Caiano is powerfully represented in photographic form in this exhibition. Its importance lies not only in its decorative merit, but also in its extraordinary symbolism. If correctly read, it may well provide one of the most important keys to our understanding of Lorenzo's thought processes at the latter end of his life. The villa was designed by Giuliano di Sangallo, and the first foundations laid in 1485. On 12th July 1490, when the powerful arcaded podium had presumably already been built, work began on the building above, a third of which is known to have been completed by 1495, when Lorenzo was already dead and his son banished. This is most likely to have been the front mass with its pedimented ionic loggia and the tympanum with the frieze (presented here in photographic form). It is likely then that the frieze itself – like Filippino Lippi's mural of the *Death of Laocöon* and the stucco barrel vaulted loggia with its lacunars also decorated by Lippi – had already been completed by the time of Lorenzo's death, or at least approved as a 'design'. Bertoldo di Giovanni, who died at the villa in 1491, is now generally held to have been commissioned to design the frieze, although two craftsmen are thought to have been responsible for its execution, Bertoldo being one of them.

The frieze is made up of five Robbianesque bas relief panels in white, blue, yellow, green and purplish brown. There have been numerous iconographical interpretations of the complex and mysterious figures, which all turn on specific references to literature and classical mythology, and Medici devices, Laurentian ones in particular. In 1991 I published a theory based on the interpretation of a Platonic myth and its important ethical significance, that I should like to take up again here. It is based on the contrast between Good and Evil, to which Lorenzo, given his notoriously two-faced character, should have been particularly sensitive, indeed "Machiavelli ... described him as harbouring two persons" (E.H. Gombrich, *Norm and Form*).

Given that this is not the right place for extensive argument or debate, I will stick to the main points of my own interpretation, which takes the *Myth of Er* in Book X of Plato's *Republic* as the philosophical 'point of departure' for the frieze. The warrior Er, awakening from a comatose sleep, described the celestial afterlife of souls which, before being reincarnated and with the assistance of Necessity and the Parcae, chose an object representative of their fate in the coming life. The souls were then accompanied by a demon or a genius representing this fate, were it just or unjust, good or bad. I shall base my interpretation of the five reliefs (which make up an organic and united whole) on the premise that they represent the effects of the prenatal choice of souls, that is to say the divergent destinies of the good soul bent on virtue and the iniquitous soul bent on vice, in five stages:

1. *The beginning of iniquitous life and righteous life*
At the centre of the relief is Nature, responsible for the generation of souls, outside a dark grotto encircled by the *ouroboros*, the serpent with its tail in its mouth. This is a Medici device representing the eternity of time, which in this context is also a metaphor for the cyclical reincarnation, or *metempsychosis* according to Plato. The souls of children flying from Nature's breast can be seen, on close examination of the original,

tightly gripping the fate (good or bad) that they have plucked for themselves from Necessity's lap, according to Er's vision. The souls, already grown and adolescent, travel towards their respective destinies, forever, accompanied by their demon-guides or genii. The two sets of children flying away from Nature are, therefore, each made up of the soul and its genius. To the right, the youth with the armillary sphere and the compass represents an orderly and just life; to the left is a life of iniquity, symbolized by the deformed old man, who according to 16th century iconography represents Vice, shaking the seven serpentine humps of the Lernaean Hydra. The elementary contrast between Good and Evil highlights the dramatic and irreversible choice that the soul has to make before it can begin a new life. The subsequent reliefs use classical mythological imagery to illustrate the effects of this choice.

2. *Iniquity and justice at the dawn of civilization*
Here the primordial antithetical couple of Saturn and Jove illustrate the contrast between the archaic brutal age of the human race, with the cruel domination of the father of the gods and the subsequent civilization of the world by his son Jove, cleverly abstracted from his father by his mother Rhea. Jove is shown being nursed by Amalthea the goat under cover of a staged battle between the Corybants, next to the Laurentian device of the six beehives and their bees. This is not just a reference to the classic *topos* of apiculture (which was practised at Poggio), but a symbol both of an ordered community reigned over by a monarch and, according to Orphic philosophy, of the swarm of souls born to the Divinity.

3. *The effect of iniquity: war*
The third and fourth relief illustrate the results or effects of both choices on the behaviour of the human race: the pursuit of Evil (war) or of Good (labour). In the centre of the third panel, which is also the centre of the frieze as a whole, is the two-faced Janus, god of the year, Time and War. He is seen guarding the doorway of his temple from which, to the priest's dismay, Mars can be seen emerging to incite his waiting troops to war. Janus is a pivotal figure in the frieze, an image that carries a great many references to Lorenzo himself. He is the god of the year and 1st January, Lorenzo's birthday, is his Day, and he can thus be regarded as "his" genius: this ambiguous *daemon* accounts for the contradictory duplicity of Lorenzo's temperament and inclination, and his authority to dictate war or peace, aspire to Good or favour Evil. It is worth mentioning that one of the most intriguing pieces in Lorenzo's vast collection of antiques was a head of Jove that appeared to be angry on one side and benevolent on the other.

4. *The effect of justice: the peaceful labours of the fields*
In the fourth panel, the Seasons regulate the serene accomplishment of the year's labours in the fields, each one carried out by the appropriate Month.

5. *Punishment and reward after death*
In the final panel, human life draws to an end and, in a return to the iconographic

drama set in the first scene, the destinies of the just soul and the unjust soul part company for ever. After death, symbolized by the two brothers Sleep and Death and their sister Oblivion, both souls mount a quadriga, which derives from the Platonic image of the biga. Arriving at a door, however, they are greeted in different ways by the custodian with a halo of sunbeams who stands guard over the entrance to the celestial kingdom. This may well be Astrea, goddess of Justice. The iniquitous charioteer, forcing the horses towards the entrance, is stopped by the goddess who determinedly takes the muzzle of one of the horses between her hands. The just charioteer, however, is beckoned through by the goddess with an expansive, encouraging gesture whereupon his horses rear up as an apotheosis.

Even the dividers between the panels, made to look like herms, of which three out of four have survived, fit in with this theory of opposing moral principles: two of them look like Hercules, positive hero, according to Pythagoras, of the just choice of virtue; the third, armed, symbolizes Mars, who inspired the unjust choice of war.

The glazed terracotta frieze commissioned by Lorenzo for the villa at Poggio occupies a position of supreme importance, both because its chronology coincides with Lorenzo's maturity and because of the solemnity of its theme: the allegory of the eternal, lacerating choice that will carry the soul either to perdition or to salvation. The risks of man's continued oscillation between these two opposing moral tendencies were well known to Lorenzo who, in his later years, surveyed the uncertain and dangerous path of his soul with distress, led as he was by an unreliable genius ("a wretched and unfriendly guide") towards an unknown destiny. I believe that the unique and innovative theme of the frieze may well have been conceived by Lorenzo himself, with some help from Marsilio Ficino as regards those aspects borrowed from Platonic doctrine. Lorenzo has left not just a profound piece of humanist culture, but an authentic scheme for a moral life which, through the vocabulary of the images, constitutes a severe warning and a serious spiritual testament.

List of Events Held in Honour of Lorenzo il Magnifico

Organized by the Committee for the Celebrations in Honour of the Fifth Centenary of the Death of Lorenzo il Magnifico

Exhibitions

Architettura di Lorenzo il Magnifico – Spedale degli Innocenti – 8th April-26th July 1992

Il disegno fiorentino del tempo di Lorenzo il Magnifico – Galleria degli Uffizi – 8th April-5th July 1992

Le tems revient. Feste e spettacoli nella Firenze di Lorenzo il Magnifico – Palazzo Medici-Riccardi – 8th April-19th July 1992

All'ombra del lauro – Biblioteca Medicea Laurenziana – 4th May-30th June 1992

Lorenzo dopo Lorenzo. La fortuna storica di Lorenzo il Magnifico – Biblioteca Nazionale Centrale di Firenze – 4th May-30th July 1992

La Chiesa e la Città a Firenze nel XV secolo – Sotterranei di San Lorenzo – 6th June-6th September 1992

Maestri e compagni del giovane Michelangiolo – Casa Buonarroti – 30th June-19th October 1992

Maestri e botteghe. Pittura a Firenze alla fine del Quattrocento – Palazzo Strozzi – 16th October 1992-10th January 1993

Il maestro di Leonardo. Il restauro dell'incredulità di S. Tommaso di Andrea Verrocchio – Palazzo Vecchio, Salone dei Cinquecento – 5th December 1992-17th April 1993

Vivere nel contado al tempo di Lorenzo il Magnifico – Villa medicea di Cafaggiolo – 19th June-27th September 1992

La sicurezza dell'esistere – Villa medicea di Cerreto Guidi – 20th June-20th September 1992

Conferences

Il disegno fiorentino al tempo di Lorenzo il Magnifico – Villa Spelman – 3rd-5th June 1992

Lorenzo il Magnifico ed il suo mondo – Villa "I Tatti" – 9th-13th June 1992

La musica a Firenze a tempo di Lorenzo il Magnifico – Dipartimento delle Arti e dello Spettacolo; Biblioteca Nazionale di Firenze – 15th-17th June 1992

La Toscana al tempo di Lorenzo il Magnifico: politica, economia, cultura, arte – Florence, Pisa, Siena – 5th-8th November 1992

Dall'Accademia neoplatonica fiorentina alla riforma – Istituto Nazionale di Studi sul Rinascimento – 30th October 1992

La cultura ebraica a Firenze all'epoca di Lorenzo il Magnifico – Accademia "La Colombaria" – 29th November 1992

Restoration works

Palazzo Medici Riccardi: Cappella dei Magi and Cortile d'onore
Orsanmichele, Bronze group of "St Thomas' Incredulity" by Andrea del Verrocchio

Itineraries through the Florentine Museums

Museo degli Argenti in Palazzo Pitti
Museo del Bargello (Eredità del Magnifico)
Museo Archeologico
Galleria degli Uffizi
.

Itineraries through the Territory

Maiano (Fiesole): Via della pietra lavorata

Mugello: Villa di Cafaggiolo, Castello del Trebbio, Convento del Bosco, Palazzo dei Vicari di Scarperia

Val di Sieve: Pontassieve, Dicomano e Vecchio, (Medici bridge, Logge del Mercato, Museo del Beato Angelico)
Trekking itinerary: Fortezza di S. Martino – Villa di Cafaggiolo

Prato (Comune): Itinerary on horseback between Cafaggiolo and Poggio a Caiano

Calenzano (Comune): Pieve di S. Donato : photographic exhibition: *Calenzano medicea. Arte sacra dalle chiese di Calenzano al tempo di Lorenzo il Magnifico*

Poggio a Caiano (Comune): Villa di Poggio a Caiano – Historical Revival – *Tutti a corte*

Cerreto Guidi (Comune): Villa di Cerreto Guidi – Exhibition – *La sicurezza dell'esistere* Guided tour of the marshes around Fucecchio

Barga: Itinerary taking in the local churches

Lunigiana: Itinerary – *La Lunigiana, chiave e porta della Tuscia*

Poggibonsi: Sangallo's Fortezza di Poggio Imperiale

Castellina in Chianti: Exhibition – *Il Magnifico e la difesa dei confini*

Badia a Coltibuono: Guided tours of the Abbey

Foiano (Val di Chiana): Exhibition – *La battaglia di Scannagallo*

Monte San Savino: Ceramics Exhibition

Val Tiberina: Exhibition of local maps

Entertainment

Gipsoteca vivente – Teatro degli Animosi, Marradi – 20th June 1992

Il Duca de' broccoli – S. Quirico a Monticelli (Florence) – 21st June 1992

Giuliano – Anfiteatro delle Cascine – 22nd and 24th June 1992

Chi vuol esser lieto sia e del doman non v'è certezza – Teatro Manzoni, Pistoia – 25th-26th June 1992

Lorenzo il Magnifico e gli anni della dinastia dei Medici al cinema – Auditorium della Regione Toscana and Cripta di San Lorenzo – 1st-7th July 1992

La congiura dei Pazzi – Centro Avviamento all'espressione – 9th-11th July 1992

La Firenze del Magnifico Lorenzo – Church of San Stefano al Ponte – 19th July 1992

Finito di stampare nel mese di ottobre 1993
dalla Amilcare Pizzi Arti Grafiche
per conto di Edizioni Charta